**Columbus, the Cannon Ball and
the Common Pump**

BOOKS BY LANCELOT HOGBEN

Mathematics for the Million
Science for the Citizen
Mathematics in the Making
From Cave Painting to Comic Strip
The Mother Tongue
The Beginnings of Science series
Volume 1   Beginnings and Blunders
Volume 2   Astronomer Priest and Ancient Mariner
Volume 3   Maps, Mirrors and Mechanics

LANCELOT HOGBEN

Columbus, the Cannon Ball and the Common Pump

HEINEMANN : LONDON

William Heinemann Ltd
15 Queen Street, Mayfair, London W1X 8BE
LONDON   MELBOURNE   TORONTO
JOHANNESBURG   AUCKLAND

First published 1974
© Lancelot Hogben 1974
SBN 434 94308 8

Filmset and printed in Great Britain by
BAS Printers Limited, Wallop, Hampshire

Contents

Acknowledgements

The author is indebted to the following for permission to reproduce illustrations: George Allen and Unwin Ltd for Figs. 25, 27, 28a, 29, 30, 32, 33, 34, 35, 36, 37, 44, 45, 46, 47, 48, 49, 50, 52, 53, 55, 56, 57, 58, 59, 60, 61, 63, 66, 67, 68, 69, 70; Augsberg Picture Library for Fig. 22; The Curators of the Bodleian Library for Fig. 14; The Trustees of the British Museum for Figs. 11, 24, 31; Clarendon Press, Oxford, for Fig. 51; Ginn and Co. Ltd for Fig. 1a; Her Majesty's Stationery Office for Fig. 54, 65; Hofmuseum, Vienna, for Fig. 9; Macmillan and Co. Ltd for Fig. 1b; Mansell Collection for Fig. 7; Max Parrish Ltd for Figs. 2, 3, 4, 5, 6, 8, 10, 13, 15, 16, 17, 18, 19, 21, 23; Rathbone Books Ltd for Figs. 28b, 64; Royal Geographical Society for Fig. 12; Royal Observatory, Greenwich, for Fig. 39; Stephens Press Picture Agency for Fig. 20; The Trustees of the Science Museum, London, for Fig. 38.

1 **Wedlock of East and West**

Two earlier volumes of the story of how science began embrace four periods of the history of civilisation. The first is associated in the western world with the perfection of the calendar by the priestly astronomers of Egypt and Iraq and with the beginnings of mathematics in the service of temple architecture, tribute and trade. Though astronomy and mathematics continued to progress in Iraq till after the conquests of Alexander, i.e. about 300 B.C., we may date our first period from 3500 to 1500 B.C.

By 1500 B.C. maritime trade had begun between Egypt, Phoenicia (Lebanon), Crete and Cyprus. As it extended its range beyond the Mediterranean, a new class of literate master mariners collated their experience of the changing aspect of the heavenly bodies as their ships sailed into more northerly and southerly latitudes. By about 500 B.C. there emerged from such experience among the sea-faring Greeks the recognition that the earth is a spherical body. In the Greek-speaking colonies and mainland, geometry and geography had reached their highest level before 300 B.C.

The scene now shifts back to Egypt and Iraq where the conquests of Alexander the Great had planted colonies of Greek veterans and scholars. This phase spanned some six centuries, roughly from 300 B.C. to A.D. 300, during which the great university founded by one of Alexander's generals in the city named after the conqueror was the centre of all learning in the west. Its main achievements were the determination of the earth's circumference and of the distance of the moon from the earth, the construction of star maps and earth maps in latitude and longitude, discovery of the geometrical laws of reflection from plane and curved mirrors, of the principle of the lever and that of buoyancy. It also brought mathematics into the service of astronomy by construction of trigonometrical tables—

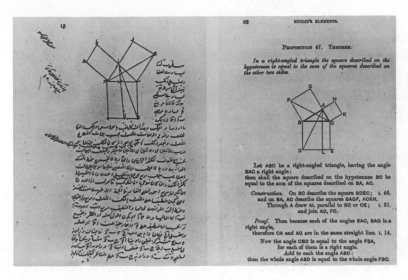

1. *At a time when most of Spain and Portugal were under Moslem rule, Euclid came into mediaeval Europe through Arabic translations.*

though not of the sort we now use.

A fourth period extending from about A.D. 500 to A.D. 1200 is the period whose main achievement comes from the Far East. This was the introduction of the symbol for zero, and therewith an immense simplification of the art of calculation. Also from India, we inherit trigonometry of a simpler type than that of the Alexandrians. The Moslem conquests of Spain and Sicily brought the Hindu-Arabic numerals to Northern and Western Europe. With them came new and simple rules of calculation. By translation into Arabic of works by Greek-speaking scholars such as Euclid (Fig. 1), Archimedes, Ptolemy and Galen, they also made possible in Baghdad a marriage between the new scholarship of the East and the major achievements of Alexandrian civilisation. Moslem astronomers and geographers improved the crude maps of the Alexandrians, providing the tools of scientific navigation for the great Portuguese and Spanish voyages of the fifteenth century of the Christian era.

We may associate each of the four phases of the earlier part of our story with a new technique of communication. If we define natural science as the written record of man's knowledge of nature, it is true to say that science is as old as the art of writing. Indeed, the most imperative and earliest need for a record arose from Man's dependence on the heavenly bodies for locating himself in space and anticipating the seasons. To keep track of the passage of time, some sort of tally, by means of strokes cut on tree trunks or chipped on stone, was indispensable. The repetitive strokes of all the earliest numerals recall this first step in the compilation of the record. We recognise them still in the Roman signs, I, II, III, etc.

The written records of the earliest temple observatories in the first phase of our story had already incorporated other signs as need arose to catalogue the priestly possessions and tribute exacted from those who tilled the soil and tended the herds. Initially, these enlisted a skill which our earliest forefathers practised on the rock surface of their caves. In short, the temple scripts were at first pictorial, though their pictorial character—other than what persists in the numeral signs—eventually became blurred beyond recognition.

The temple observatory fixed the study of astronomy in the strait-jacket of a stationary site which excluded the opportunity to witness the changing face of the sky in more northerly and southerly latitudes; and the clumsiness of the tools of communication of the astronomer priest prevented the spread of literacy beyond its precincts. In Egypt, a battery of different symbols for each word made enormous demands on the memory and on the duration of education of the temple scribe who kept its records on light and portable scrolls of papyrus. In Iraq, where the symbols underwent considerable simplification to represent sound rather than meaning, the writing surface was a tablet of soft clay, afterwards baked in the sun. A temple library would have to be of tremendous size to accommodate a single issue of the *New York Times*, if produced on such material. It was thus an immense advantage when Greek-speaking merchant mariners took from their Semitic trade rivals the new and vastly more economical method of alphabetic writing, and from the Egyptians, with whom they exchanged their wares, the compact and portable writing surface called papyrus. Thus came the ancient mariner into the picture of infant science.

Albeit the gateway to a wider literacy, the advent of the alphabet turned out to be a mixed blessing. Though the earlier numerals of the temple scribe were bulky on account of the repetitive principle, they were at least explicit. The use of alphabetic signs (e.g. Roman V, X, L, C, D, M) was of itself unobjectionable if, as in early Greek and in Roman script, used only to distinguish *decimal* (or *quinary**) orders of magnitude. Later Greek traders and mathematicians followed the Hebrew practice of assigning a number to each letter of the alphabet, thus adding formidably to the load on the memory entailed in calculation. It also made algebra as we know it now an unattainable aspiration. The Alexandrian mathematicians and astronomers thus inherited a handicap which must have greatly limited the number of scholars skilled in the art of calculation. They did, however, borrow from the temple civilisations of Iraq a system of representing fractions which had some merit. This *sexagesimal* representation in multiples of 60 persists today in our division of angles into degrees and of the hour into minutes and seconds.

Introduction of the symbol for zero and reduction of all other numeral signs to nine by the Hindus was an immensely valuable improvement of man's tools of com-

* Roman numerals are partly *decimal* orders, i.e. in *tens*, hundreds, and thousands (X, C, M), partly *quinary* (i.e. in fives), e.g. V, L and D.

2. *At the beginning of the fifteenth century, European pilots relied on manuals of navigation copied by hand on parchment. Here is a leaf from one such manual setting forth how to determine latitude by the altitude of the Pole Star which then described a circle of 3° round the Celestial Pole.*

munication. Its immediate benefit was the formulation of rules for calculation within the reach of any child with the opportunity to learn, and hence more speedy performance of astronomical computations of use to pilots exploring hitherto unfamiliar ocean routes. By depriving alphabetic signs of specific numeral values, it cleared the way in the fullness of time for algebra as we know it today.

However, two circumstances restricted the spread of these benefits until we approach the Great Navigations of the fifteenth century of our own era. Before then, the Rutter Books, i.e. navigation manuals (Fig. 2) for the pilot and primers of the new arithmetic (then called *algorithms*) for use in the newly endowed so-called *grammar schools*, were copied by hand on parchment. Both the cost of the material used and the labour of copying entailed an expense which the introduction of two Chinese inventions —paper and printing—vastly reduced. This revolution in man's means of communication was so important an antecedent to the efflorescence of science in the sixteenth and seventeenth centuries of our era that it deserves more than a passing remark. It will serve as a fitting introduction to our survey in the next chapter of other inventions which contributed to scientific progress in the wake of the first fleets of large ships to cross the Atlantic.

2 **Five Centuries of Incubation**

Hindu mathematics and Moslem geography had reached their highest level by about A.D. 1000. Between that date and the exploration of the New World, there was little advance of scientific knowledge in the usual sense of the word. It was a period of incubation during which many inventions new to European civilisation were destined to contribute to an explosive outburst of scientific curiosity and discovery during the two centuries after the Columbian voyages.

Among all the inventions of this period of incubation, paper and printing take pride of place. Within little more than a generation after the printing press came from Germany to Italy, and then to England, there appeared illustrated—some beautifully so—treatises on human anatomy, metallurgy and mining, artillery and astronomy. From the start, the new presses produced text-books of commercial arithmetic for the trader, nautical almanacs for the navigator and trigonometrical tables for the surveyor and astronomer. Never before in the history of mankind had knowledge of the world's work been so accessible to the scholar, and never before had the useful fruits of scholarship been more accessible to people engaged in fruitful work.

During the first century A.D., the Chinese may have learned from the wasp an important lesson. This insect makes a papery nest by chewing vegetable fibre. Following its example, the Chinese used any vegetable material to hand, such as old nets, rags or worn out rope. This they macerated in tubs and then put it through a sieve. If compressed to required thickness, the fibres adhere when dry. This is a much cheaper writing surface than parchment or vellum, made from stretched, pressed and dried animal membranes and at one time the only writing surface known in Europe. The recipe for paper making was

presumably acquired by the Arabs when they captured
Samarkand in A.D.750 and it arrived in Europe about A.D.
1200, with the Moslem invasions of Spain and Sicily.
During the next three centuries, water mills which could
supply the power for macerating and compressing the
raw materials for paper making spread throughout
Christendom (Fig. 3) to meet the need for cleaning wool
and preventing flooding of mines.

3. *During the century
before printing began
in Europe, the water
mill had been har-
nessed to expedite
manufacture of paper.*

In China, whence Europe learned to use the silk worm,
stamping coloured patterns on silk was a practice as early
as paper making. Such stamping of coloured patterns on
pottery is of vast antiquity and readers of the second
instalment of *The Beginnings of Science* (*Astronomer Priest
and Ancient Mariner*) will recall how the priestly astrono-

mers of Iraq in 3000 B.C. were using a wedge-shaped punch to impress their script symbols on soft clay tablets afterwards baked in the sun. About A.D. 700, or even earlier, the technique of stamping charms on paper by wood blocks began in China (Fig. 4), where the production of playing cards produced in the same way soon followed.

4. *On the right an eleventh century Chinese playing card. On the left an early fifteenth century European example of the* Heiligen *sold at the shrines of saints. This one portrays St Florian, protector against fire. Both the above were printed from wood blocks.*

The first samples of printing by wood blocks in Europe are also playing cards (Fig. 5). A prohibition against the use of playing cards by artisans during working hours issued by the Provost of Paris in 1397 was one of many such in German towns. Books with woodblock illustrations followed suit; and there survive a few books in which the text had been impressed by letters carved on such blocks (Fig. 6).

Needless to say, carving the same letters in relief again and again on a wood block was a time-consuming process; but materials for an alternative procedure were already to hand. By A.D. 1400 there were now two bodies of wealthy craftsmen—jewellers and armourers—skilled in the art of using punches and dies to make patterns in relief on a metal surface. Indeed, before A.D. 1300 metal founders knew the art of using stamps, each with a single letter to

5. *Fifteenth century French playing cards printed in colour from wood blocks.*

make an impression for molten metal in soft sand to appear in relief on the casting of bells, coins and pewter vessels (Fig. 7). Thus there were the means available for

6. *Two pages from a fifteenth century devotional book printed from wood blocks.*

making *movable type*, i.e. metal casts of individual letters which could be used over and over again when enough copies of a book had been through the screw presses (Fig. 8) which paper manufacturers and printers had learned to use from the wine producer (Fig. 9).

Considerable advances in the techniques of painting could now make a vital contribution to the printer's art.

7. *Among the artificers whose skill contributed to movable type were those who made bells for churches and other public buildings.*

8. *An early printing press using movable type.*

One such was that European artists of the fourteenth century had already begun to use vegetable oils as a medium in which to suspend a pigment. Before then, painters had used water-soluble dyes stiffened with egg-white. Such a recipe was suitable for making an ink which would adhere to a wood block; but it would be useless if applied to a metal surface. Thus the painter's contribution to the new invention was the provision of a suitable ink for the type. It also made possible a better technique of engraving than that from wood blocks. Instead of smearing sticky ink on a raised surface, it was now possible to get the same result by filling the crevices in a metal plate wiped clean. In such a setting, the goldsmith and the silversmith, well versed in the uses of imprinting a pattern, could make common cause with the artist illustrator of the printed word.

9. *When printing began in Europe, the wine trade already employed presses essentially like the manually operated ones of the earliest printers.*

Printing from movable type started in Germany a little less than fifty years before Columbus first sailed into an unknown West. The year 1445 seems to date a single extant leaf of a poem from the press of the pioneer master printer Gutenberg of Strasbourg, himself financed by a goldsmith of Mainz; and it is certain that printing from movable type was on the wing within ten years from this date in several German cities. German printers brought the art to Rome in 1467 and two years later, also with the patronage of a goldsmith, to Venice. Caxton set up his press in England in 1476 and produced the first book printed in English a year later.

One example suffices to put the spotlight on what this meant in terms of available written matter to satisfy the appetite of a growing body of literate master craftsmen, navigators, merchants and bankers in the ports and cities of Italy, Germany, Britain and France. Before there was printing on paper from movable type, only very wealthy people could own books. About 50 years earlier, an Italian prince hired forty-five copyists to equip his

10. Right *Page of an early German commercial arithmetic dated 1489.*
Left *Page of English commercial arithmetic—Robert Record's* Whetstone of Witte *dated 1557.*

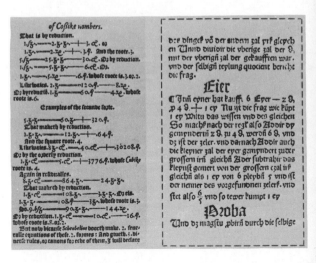

private library. By working hard for nearly two years, these men produced only two hundred volumes. Production of a single copy of one book would then keep a scrivener busy for several months; but seventy years after Gutenberg set up his press, a partly political, partly religious, book written in Germany by Martin Luther sold no less than 4000 copies in five days. A century earlier it would have taken several thousand men to produce so many copies in the same time.

The impact of printing on the spread of the new art of calculation (Fig. 10) and that of map making (Figs. 11 and 12), as also availability of tables for the use of the navigator, of the surveyor and of the astronomer who could find a wealthy patron, calls for no further comment. One cannot, however, dismiss the significance of the partnership between painter and printer without mention of two of its early masterpieces. Such was the tempo of change that they appeared within little more than a century of the beginning of the new book trade. One was the *De Fabrica Humani Corporis*[1] of Vesalius (1543) which came out in the same year as the *De Revolutionibus Orbium Celestium*[2] of Copernicus. The other was the *De*

[1] i.e. Concerning the Structure of the Human Body.
[2] i.e. Concerning the Revolutions of the Heavenly Bodies.

Re Metallica[3] of Georg Agricola (1553). The illustrations of both are superbly informative, without parallel in the previous history of mankind (Figs. 13–16).

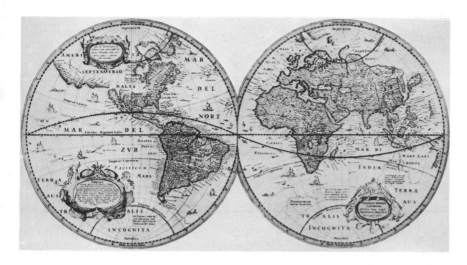

11 & 12. Early printed maps based on information brought back from the great voyages of the fifteenth and sixteenth centuries.

[3] i.e. Concerning Things Metallic.

13. *An illustration from the* De Re Metallica *of Agricola showing use of water power to raise heavy loads.*

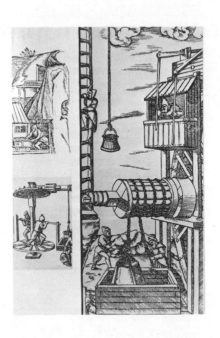

Because of papal prohibition of dissection of the human body, the study of human anatomy languished in mediaeval Christendom except where Jewish missionaries of Moslem culture enjoyed tolerance through influence of monastic orders, as founders of hospitals and custodians of the monastery physic gardens, dedicated to the care of the sick. Where there was instruction in anatomy, the authority was Galen (A.D. 130–200), physician to the emperor Marcus Aurelius and last of the Alexandrian anatomists. Provided with no explanatory, or very inferior, diagrams (Fig. 14), teachers and students who pored over the hand-copied manuscripts of his treatise could argue inconclusively about the precise meaning of the text. When, therefore, that of Vesalius appeared, with ample engravings by a pupil of the illustrious painter Titian, the event initiated a new era in the history of medicine. A new interest in the human body enlisted painters and draughtsmen as participators in its faithful portrayal. Leonardo da Vinci bequeathed to posterity some 750 anatomical

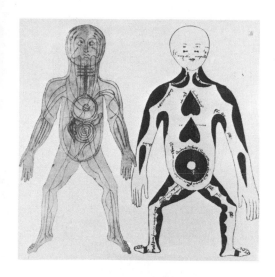

14. *Illustration from a manual of human anatomy hand copied before printing from movable type began.*

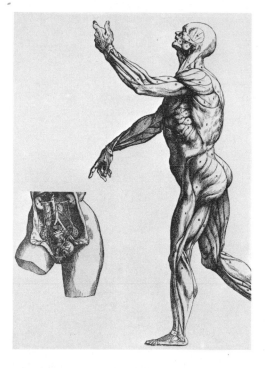

15. *Contrast the foregoing illustration with this specimen from the* De Fabrica Humani Corporis *of Vesalius printed in 1543.*

sketches never published in his lifetime. He had planned a treatise on the human body; but he did not complete it.

If only because of its illustrations, Agricola's treatise brought for the first time mining technology, and therewith the uses of the common pump, to the attention of scholars whose university training steeped in Aristotle's superstitions had not completely extinguished curiosity. Its impact on scientific thought had scarcely ceased to be salutary a century after it first appeared. A century later than that, the new realism of the great Italian painters was to infuse new life into botanical classification (Fig. 17).

Nor was it only in virtue of their services as illustrators that the birth of a new style of painting in Italy during the century before printing from movable type contributed to the great scientific awakening which followed. True perspective, i.e. the practice of using a single vanishing point for all straight lines irrespective of the plane section

16. *Frontispiece of Vesalius' treatise on human anatomy, showing a professor demonstrating dissection of a human cadaver to his students.*

17. *The right-hand bottom figure taken from a thirteenth century Anglo-Norman herbal fancifully pictures the Centaury plant. To the left, the violet from a herbal printed in 1530 demonstrates the contribution of the artist to the first herbals to appear in print. The pictures of ivy and bramble are from John Gerard's herbal which was first printed in 1597.*

of a picture (Fig. 18) was non-existent alike in West and East before the end of the fourteenth century. It was the outcome of painstaking investigation into the laws of optics, to which Leonardo da Vinci (1452–1519), one of its outstanding practitioners, made a noteworthy contribution. Drawings by Albrecht Dürer (about 1526) exhibit the artist (Fig. 19) in the role of investigator, disclosing what devices he used to further the stereoscopic illusion.

Artists of the fifteenth and sixteenth centuries contributed to the advance of science in another way with less immediate pay-off. In their search for new pigments, they were among the few clients from whom the alchemist gained a market for pure compounds at a time when the major manufacturing industries, other than metallurgical, relied on such crude raw materials as chalk, sand, charcoal, pot-ashes, sea-salt, kelp and saltpetre.

18. *This painting of the Last Supper by Leonardo da Vinci (about 1494) is a superb example of perspective, in his time an innovation.*

19. *This wood-cut of 1525 by Dürer shows apparatus being used for perspective drawing.*

Coloured glass beads are among the relics of the earliest civilisations, and the much admired glass vessels of the Romans owe their charm at least partly to the fact that they were not truly transparent. Though clear panes have been found in the ruins of Roman palaces built in the last two centuries of the Western Empire and ornate coloured glass windows for churches flourished after Christianity became the state religion in its Eastern realm, there was no compelling need for windows to protect the urban house-holder from the cold while European civilisation was confined to the warm South. As civilisation spread north-wards to Germany, Normandy and Britain between A.D. 1100 and 1400, the emergence of a prosperous class of bankers, merchants and craftsmen in a colder, windier climate created a new demand. While we still find open slits in the castles of the contemporary robber barons (Fig. 20), the wealthier townsmen of the chartered boroughs have windows with transparent glass panes, or at least bottle glass of greenish hue joined by leaden strips (Fig. 21). In 1474 Breslau had windows of clear glass, parch-ment and bladder to keep out the cold.

20. *Baronial castle with open-slit windows. By day, only in bright sunlight, and standing close to the slit crevices which served as windows of these feudal castles, could one study a parchment manuscript. They had however other uses. The stench of excrement and, at night, smoke from the torches and log fires of the banquet-ing hall would have been intolerable had there been no such means of ventilation.*

21. *Scene from a four-*
teenth century city
showing the glass
windows of shops
and houses where
the prosperous
merchants and
craftsmen dwelt.

In short, the demands of climate encouraged the production of glass of high transparency; and glass-making,
as an essential domestic building craft, created a demand
greatly in excess of its use for ornament. By A.D. 1600
availability of cheap transparent glass, which one could
fashion to make tubes and flasks, placed at the disposal of
the scientific investigator entirely new tools for the
measurement of gas volume and pressure as well as vessels
in which chemical processes are open to inspection.
Without glass tubing, two inventions of vast importance,
both made before 1650, would have been impossible. One
was the thermometer, the other the barometer.

Among new manufactures of our period of incubation,
other than paper and clear glass for windows, those which
were to influence the future of natural science most
powerfully were gunpowder, clocks and spectacles (Fig.
22). Gunpowder, like paper, was a Chinese invention and
it is likely that knowledge of it reached Europe, as did
paper, in the wake of the Moslem conquests, though some
English patriots assert that an English monk, Roger Bacon,

discovered it independently in about A.D. 1250. Be that as it may, there were powder mills in Europe a century before the first voyage of Columbus to the New World. By then, artillery had penetrated naval warfare and use of siege artillery (Fig. 23) had greatly diminished the defensive value of feudal castles and walled city fortifications. Thus a new technological challenge had emerged. Hitherto, marksmanship by bow and arrow or the use of the javelin relied on individual skill derived from practice. At what angle one mounted a gun to ensure that the cannon ball hit its target had now become literally a matter of life or death. As we shall later see (Chapter 6), Galileo's solution of the problem was the birth of a new science.

22. *Sixteenth century portrait showing the use of spectacles to make reading possible for those who are long-sighted through age.*

When one recalls that Ptolemy and his contemporaries (about A.D. 200) performed experiments on refraction of light, and that the formation of images by concave and convex mirrors had been established four centuries earlier, the appearance of spectacles on the stage of history more than a thousand years after Ptolemy's death would be difficult to explain without the knowledge that cheap transparent glass had not been available much before that time. Our earliest information about the use of glass to magnify objects is that Al Hazen, a Moslem scholar, used a segment of a glass sphere as a lens. At a later date, Roger Bacon in his *Opus Majus* (1266) knew

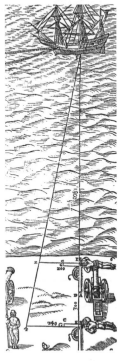

23. *Illustrations from a manual of artillery by Tartaglia printed in 1585.*

how to magnify writing by placing the segment of a sphere of glass with its plane surface on the page of a manuscript. An Italian portrait painted in 1352 shows a cardinal with two mounted lenses riveted together and fixed before his eyes.

The inventor of spectacles seems to have been an Italian in about the year A.D. 1300. Solicitous monks popularised the device for the benefit of "poor blind men" meaning probably to compensate for extremely long sight due to old age. The invention of printing thus gave a new impetus to its manufacture. Owing to such long-sightedness (*presbyopia*) nearly all people past a certain age are incapable of reading even a newspaper without the aid of spectacles (Fig. 22). Needless to say, the commercial production of lenses created a new field of scientific enquiry into image formation by refraction. It also brought in its train two instruments which were to revolutionise man's knowledge of the universe. One was the telescope. The other was the microscope.

For the future of science, not least important of the inventions of our period of incubation was that of the wheel-driven clock. Just as the open slit windows of the feudal castles were incompatible with a high standard of efficiency and comfort when trade and industry spread into the grey northern climates of Germany, the Netherlands, Normandy and Britain, the sundial was no longer adequate to time-keeping in the same setting, and there was no longer the local know-how to construct water-clocks like the remarkable model invented by Ctesibius at Alexandria in the third century B.C.

By becoming the official religion of the Roman Empire during the reign of Constantine, the christian church had necessarily assumed the responsibility of time-keeping, hitherto the prerogative of its priestly predecessors. Within the monasteries and abbeys each hour of the day had its appointed ritual or duty, and it was in this context that clocks geared with toothed wheels driven by the falling of a weight made their first appearance about A.D. 1000. In England, the earliest public clock was erected in A.D. 1288. These primitive weight driven clocks were not very reliable by modern standards (Fig. 36). Builders did not instal the Moorish type of sundial we see so often on church towers in north-western Europe as a means of telling the time at any hour of the day. As such, they would have been useless when the sky was, as so often, overcast. Their function was to correct the vagaries of the clock whenever the weather was propitious. Till about the date when printing from movable type began in Germany, the only secular market for the sale of the weight-driven clock was for installation on public buildings such as the Guild (Town) Hall.

Watches—very bulky by modern standards—came into use shortly after the invention of the mainspring by a German (about A.D. 1500). Named after his home town Nuremberg Eggs (Fig. 24), they first appear in England during the reign of Henry VIII, i.e. within fifty years of the date last mentioned. Their use by the astronomer in

24. *A Nuremberg Egg —one of the first portable watches. Unfortunately a protective lid obscures the clock face.*

forecasting eclipses, occultations (see p. 33) and conjunctions of planets was immediate. In the generation which preceded the publication of the work of Copernicus on the motion of the planets, Walther of Nuremberg equipped what was to have been the first observatory with wheel-driven clocks. As our story will unfold, clock technology played a role not less important than the telescope's in the advance of astronomy during the next two centuries.

The progress of mining technology (Fig. 25) during the period A.D. 1000–1500 is relevant to the subsequent outburst of scientific curiosity and discovery less because of any new inventions it can boast of than because of a new use which it found for an invention of great antiquity. Deep shaft mining had been practised in Egypt and in China long before the Christian era. In Egypt, and elsewhere in antiquity, the labour force was made up of slaves, usually captives of war, and life was then cheap. There was thus little incentive to technological advance, and what went on in the mines did not intrude into the experience of the educated élite. When European coal mining was in its infancy during the three centuries before

25. *Two prints from Agricola's Treatise on mining technology (1556). The lower shows one ventilation device. The upper shows the use of wind power to keep a flow of air through the mine shaft.*

the Columbian voyages, we encounter a very different state of affairs in the tin mines of Britain. The miner, a free man, is the aristocrat of mediaeval labour. As such, he is alert to the hazards of explosion and suffocation; and the climate in the minefields of northern Europe exposes him to the hazards of flooding. Against this he can protect himself only by pumping out water which enters the shafts. In doing so, he makes a discovery of great theoretical as well as practical importance. It is possible to raise water by the pressure of air only a little more than thirty feet. To work profitably at a depth of 300 feet, he must, as portrayed in Agricola's treatise, have relays of pumps each placed vertically (Fig. 67) at different heights.

When we come to the rediscovery that air has weight, we shall see how significant this picture is. Here, we may also note that Agricola devotes one volume of his treatise to the health and accidents of miners, a theme that could capture no enthusiasm when life was still cheap and slave labour expendable. It is scarcely too much to say that the pictorial content of Agricola's treatise, aided and abetted by the threat of an invading North Sea to Holland and East Anglia where pumping was the price of survival, brought pump consciousness to a hitherto cloistered class of scholars. The consequences of this to mechanics, physiology and chemistry will be disclosed more fully at a later stage of our story.

The health hazards of the miner in connexion with ventilation raised several new problems, such as why some air is explosive, and some air unfit to sustain life. Their solution was eventually to prove the beginnings of a science of chemistry as we know it today. They also entailed a new approach to the nature of respiration. When the mechanism of the common pump was rightly understood, the traditional belief that respiration allows the vital spirits to escape from the body ceased to be credible. It could now be seen that our chest movements are a mechanical device to ensure that the spongy cavities of the lungs, whose thin walls are abundantly supplied with blood vessels, receive a constant supply of fresh air. To complete the picture, we have the belated recognition, partially by Servetus (1546) and more completely by Harvey (1628), that the heart itself is a pump.

In the five centuries of incubation which span the period A.D. 600–1500, two crafts other than those of the clockmaker, the maker of spectacles, the mining engineer and the manufacturer of artillery deserve mention. As we shall see later (p. 39), those who made and merchandised the mariner's compass laid the foundations for the study of terrestrial magnetism, and one may surmise that the proliferation of new musical instruments contributed to the revival of scientific interest in acoustics during the first half of the seventeenth century. At least, it provided a favourable mental climate for renewed curiosity about the propagation of sound.

Piped instruments with a keyboard date from the early part of the Alexandrian episode (i.e. third century B.C.); but their use for church music led to considerable improvements between A.D. 1000 and 1500. We may place at some date earlier than A.D. 1404 and later than 1323 the invention of stringed instruments with a keyboard. Successive models severally designated the clavichord, spinet, virginals and harpsichord followed in rapid succession between 1400 and 1550, but the modern pianoforte does not belong to our period. The first of its kind were constructed about 1700.

Throughout each stage of the story of *The Beginnings of Science,* we have been learning how new means of communication have speeded up the advance of scientific knowledge. In particular, we have already seen how important was the introduction of the alphabet and of the Hindu-Arabic numerals, and in this chapter we take up the story at a new level with the introduction of printing and of spectacles for the long-sighted elderly. In more recent times, within the last two hundred years, other technological inventions have led the way to a still larger literacy and the means of enlisting more talent in the pursuit of scientific knowledge.

A second lesson from the way the wasp builds its home suggested making paper on a larger scale and at less cost than as hitherto from old rags, first by the use of grass and, more recently, from the sawdust of lumber mills and from pulped waste paper. Mechanical printing came in the wake of steam power and linotype machine printing within the lifetime of some still living. Thus vastly cheaper reading matter, once available only for the prosperous, came within the grasp of a far wider public.

Other technological advances have made far more time

available for study of the written word. Two centuries ago, the rich relied on candles, the poor on rush light or lamps with a horizontal wick, as from a more remote antiquity than the parable of the wise virgins. Kerosene lamps with upright wicks came early in the nineteenth century. Towards its end, came electric light. This made it possible to build large hotels where there had been wayside inns or small restaurants in the towns. It also made possible the expansion of education by night classes, so that persons employed in the daytime could now study at night.

3 **Westward Ho**

While religious superstition suppressed geographical knowledge in the monasteries and attendant grammar schools of Europe during the thirteenth century of our era, a literate class of mariners brought wealth to the mercantile republics of north Italy and maintained contact with the Byzantine rump of the Eastern Roman Empire with headquarters in what is now Istanbul, *alias* Byzantium, *alias* Constantinople. How far Genoese ships traded or ventured beyond the Strait of Gibraltar we do not know. Mercantile shipping corporations then guarded their secrets jealously.

It is not unlikely that Italian trading vessels were familiar with part of the Atlantic coast of North Africa well before the fifteenth century. By that time, some at least had at their fingertips the new geographical lore of the Moslem world. Indeed, it may well be true that they had projected a round-the-Cape route to India, and that their achievements in the domain of remunerative seafaring stimulated the enthusiasm, doubtless also exciting the envy, of their first successful competitors, the Portuguese.

In 1415, under the command of his third surviving son Henry, John I, King of Portugal, had wrested from its Moslem occupants Ceuta on the African side of the Strait of Gibraltar. This operation was a springboard for the colonisation of Madeira and the exploration of the Azores. In the execution of the programme, Prince Henry gained possession of information concerning Moslem trade along the West African coast. That it was a possible source of gold is a more likely explanation of his subsequent behaviour than the official legend according to which he hoped to find a lost limb of Christendom under the rule of a legendary Prester (i.e. presbyter or priest) John.

Be that as it may, he built an observatory about the year 1420 on a headland near Cape St Vincent, the extreme South West limit of Europe. Here, he set up a school for navigators under a teacher, Master Jacome, from Majorca. For forty years the sailor Prince devoted himself to astronomical and geographical studies while equipping expeditions which earned for him the title Henry the Navigator. For preparation of maps and instruments, he recruited Moorish and Jewish experts, skilled in the newest advances of Moslem learning in the several sciences which minister to seamanship, and employed them as instructors for captains and pilots for his vessels. Thus the personnel of his expeditions had what were then the latest instruments (Fig. 29) for measuring the altitude of celestial bodies and for making other observations useful to the navigator.

Prince Henry died before a Portuguese expedition achieved one of the goals of his ambition. It reached (1482) the coast of Ghana (formerly Gold Coast) and there established (1483) what was to be the first and most magnificent of the slave-trade forts, built at El Mina (Figs. 26 A and B) with stone carried as ballast on the return journey. One of the captains of his fleet engaged in this venture, was a young man of Genoese birth, by name Christopher Columbus. Before enlisting under Henry, he had accompanied voyages by Genoese traders to Bristol. According to one source, he had visited Iceland, where he may have heard of the success of Leif Ericsson's voyage to Vinland (Fig. 27), now located alternatively on the coast of New England or on that of Nova Scotia. Seemingly, Bristol merchants at that time believed in the existence of land far to the west of Ireland. Indeed, it was from Bristol that John Cabot, another Italian seaman, sailed to the mainland of Canada in 1497 under the patronage of the

26a. *View from the sea of El Mina fort built in 1483 by the Portuguese.*

26b. *A modern view of the interior of El Mina after the Dutch had made it their stronghold for the overseas slave trade.*

English king, Henry VII.

The first two fleets of Columbus (1492 and 1493) dropped anchor in the islands of the Caribbean, i.e. Bahamas, Cuba and Haiti. He did not set foot on the mainland itself till 1498. On the whole, recent research discredits the claim that Amerigo Vespucci, who gave his name to the continent, anchored off the mainland in his first voyage of a year earlier. There is, however, little reason to doubt that John Cabot reached the coast of Nova Scotia in 1497, thus sighting the mainland of North America in a latitude midway between the regions identified by posterity as the Vinland of the Saga.

Such westerly courses signalise the challenge of a new

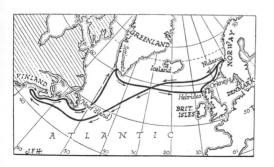

27. *The route of one of the Norse voyages from Iceland to North America about A.D. 1000.*

technological need. Long distance voyages of antiquity beyond the Mediterranean had followed a north-south course, venturing from the nearest coast only so far as the sight of familiar sea birds gave them assurance. Recognition by latitude was therefore adequate for the needs of the pilot. In short, there was no urgent need to locate the port of call by longitude. Had there been such a need, there would have been no way of satisfying it successfully.

Some readers of this book will recall (Fig. 28) that 15° of terrestrial longitude separate two places where times of transit of the same heavenly body (e.g. that of the sun at noon) differ by one hour. To determine one's longitude, all one therefore needs nowadays is a seaworthy clock (i.e. one which neither gains nor loses time appreciably throughout a long sea voyage) with a map or catalogue showing the Right Ascensions (Fig. 44) of stars. One sets the clock by noon at a place on the meridian arbitrarily chosen as the zero of longitude (now that of Greenwich by international agreement). If we call the reading of this clock *standard time*, we can now determine the longitude of any locality by the standard time of local noon by day or local transit of any bright star by night. Thus, if local noon occurs at 9 a.m. standard time we are 3 times 15° East of Greenwich, i.e. on the meridian 45° East. In 1532, less than forty years after the invention of Nuremberg Eggs (p. 23), a Dutchman, Gemma Frisius,

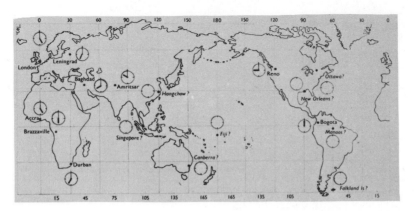

28. Above *Longitude* and Below *Local Time*.

suggested this simple recipe which set clock manufacturers a problem not solved till two centuries later (p. 44).

When their ships cast anchor to take bearings in longitude, pilots of the expeditions of Columbus and Cabot trained in the Portuguese tradition, many of them Jews having close links with Moslem centres of scientific study, could not as yet take advantage of Nuremberg Eggs to check local time from determination of the last noon. They did, however, have instruments (Fig. 29) for making angular measurements of celestial bodies, and in all probability for measuring time by the hour-glass, better than any available to the mariner when Ptolemy made the first maps bequeathed by antiquity to posterity.

To determine longitude at a port of call, the pilots of the Columbian voyages had to rely on forecasts of Celestial Signals at some standard locality, e.g. Nuremberg or Florence (Fig. 30). Besides eclipses of sun or moon, such

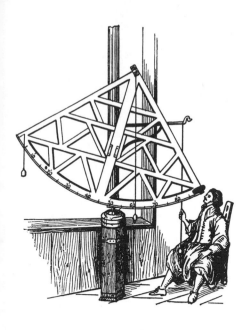

29. *Sixteenth century instrument (*Quadrant*) for measuring zenith distances. Before the invention of the vernier, the only way of making an angular measurement more accurate was to increase the size of the instrument. The astronomer Tycho Brahe used a quadrant radius 19 ft. On such a scale a difference of 1° was equivalent to approximately 4 inches.*

signals included occultations of planets or bright stars, i.e. occasions when the moon's disc covers one of them, and *conjunctions* of the moon and a planet, i.e. when each was on the same meridian of Right Ascension (Fig. 44) or celestial longitude (p. 47), but not, as in an occultation, also on the same circle of declination (Fig. 44).
At a time when predictions for periods longer than a

30. *Use of local time of celestial signals for determining longitude.* Above: *lunar eclipse.* Below: *conjunction of moon and planet.*

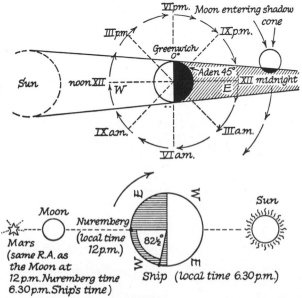

return Atlantic voyage were not likely to be very reliable, day to day forecasts had to be available. Nautical almanacs forecasting eclipses, conjunctions and occultations were not available before printing from movable type began. It is indeed highly significant that long-distance westerly navigation began in the half-century following printing, and that nautical almanacs were prominent among the first-fruits of printing from movable type.

A few examples will bring to life the way in which Columbus and his contemporaries responded to so new a challenge. On 13 January 1493, Columbus himself sought a port off Haiti where he could anchor to observe at rest the conjunction of sun and moon. On the 1493 voyage, he anchored again to observe the opposition of Jupiter and the moon, i.e. when the moon's celestial longitude differed from that of Jupiter by 180°. In 1499, Amerigo Vespucci determined the difference of longitude between Venezuela and Cadiz by observing a lunar eclipse. On another occasion he observed a conjunction of Mars and the moon. In February and April of 1520, the best trained pilot of Magellan's expedition, which was first to round the southernmost tip of South America, made similar observations according to instructions drawn up by the astronomer Faleiro, who had composed a treatise on methods for determination of longitude with a view to use on this voyage. Details of one incident of this sort must suffice to satisfy the curiosity of the reader.

When his ship was in latitude 10°N, presumably therefore near the Gulf of Venezuela, Amerigo Vespucci obtained his longitude in the following way (Fig. 30). At 7.30 p.m. local time, i.e. $7\frac{1}{2}$ hours after local noon, the moon was 1° east of Mars. At midnight by local time, it was $5\frac{1}{2}$° east, having therefore retreated in its orbit through $4\frac{1}{2}$° in the same number of hours. It should therefore have been in conjunction with Mars at 6.30 p.m. local time. A nautical almanac prepared by the German astronomer Johannes Muller, usually referred to by his Latin pseudonym as Regiomontanus, forecast a conjunction of Mars and the moon on the same date at midnight by Nuremberg time. When the time was 12.00 midnight at Nuremberg, it was therefore 6.30 p.m. at the ship's position; and local time at the ship's station was $5\frac{1}{2}$ hours behind that of Nuremberg. On the assumption that the time interval was correct, and that the almanac calculation was reliable, this would make the difference of longitude between the ship's location and Nuremberg $5\frac{1}{2} \times 15° = 82\frac{1}{2}°$. Since Nuremberg is $11°$ east of Greenwich, his longitude in modern terms was $71\frac{1}{2}°$W.

The assumption that the almanac was reliable throws light on the importance of being able to make long term forecasts of the positions of the planets. Actually, the elaborate mathematical treatment of their motions based on the teaching of Eudoxus and adopted by Hipparchus and Ptolemy, that is to say, on the assumption that the planets like the sun, moon and fixed stars revolve around the earth, could yield reliable forecasts over only very short periods. A more reliable method of computing their whereabouts was thus a necessity for westerly navigation beyond the sight of familiar sea fowl. At a time when there were no computing machines, no slide rules nor even tables of logarithms to reduce the labour of keeping astronomical tables up to date, it was also important to devise a method which sidestepped the need for laborious arithmetical exploits. That of Copernicus had the advantage of being immensely more simple than that of Ptolemy.

When Copernicus (1543) published the first detailed treatment of planetary motion from the alternative point of view, which places the sun at the centre of the solar system, there were available no new facts to discredit the earlier earth-centred view point. Support for his treatment of planetary motion gained ground only because it provided a more satisfactory solution of a problem then by no means a matter of academic interest. In so far as it postulated that the orbits of the planets are circular in contradistinction to elliptical, the Copernican treatment was indeed too simple. None the less, error involved in treating those of Venus and Mars (p. 54) in this way is not very great. His successors were not slow to make the appropriate correction. The refinement of his work by Tycho Brahe and Kepler relegated the Ptolemaic system to the limbo of discredited hypotheses because the alternative could yield far more reliable long-range forecasts of planetary positions with an immense economy of effort.

Reference to the tables of Regiomontanus (p. 35) puts the spotlight both on the search for a better formula for forecasting the behaviour of planets and on the pivotal importance of the printing press in the background of the Columbian voyages. We first hear of him as joint author in a revision of the available astronomical tables based on the work of Ptolemy. In 1461, he visited Italy to study Greek texts of the work of the latter circulating among refugees from Constantinople lately occupied by the Turks; and he published the first compendious trigono-metrical tables available in Europe other than those based on Ptolemy's writings. After he settled at Nuremberg, his pupil and wealthy patron Bernhard Walther equipped an observatory for him in which he made the first compre-hensive observations on what we now call Halley's Comet. What is of special interest about the role of printing in the context of early trans-Atlantic navigation is that Walther also equipped him with a printing press for the publication of astronomical tables. In 1474 he issued a volume of these covering the period 1474–1506.

The same treatise sets out in detail instructions for using observations on the moon's position as a means of determining longitude at sea. This so-called method of *lunar distances* was to engage Newton's interest two centuries later. It depends on the fact that the moon completes a revolution in its orbit, i.e. relative to the fixed stars, in a *sidereal* month of $27\frac{1}{2}$ days. It therefore moves through a mean angle of slightly over $1°$ in two hours. Since its Declination (p. 48) as well as its Right Ascension changes in the course of a revolution, the calculation of its angular displacement with reference to any single fixed star is complicated, and the usefulness of the computation depends on both the sensitivity of the measuring device and the reliability of tables showing its location at different times of the day and on different days of the year.

Search for a reliable way of determining longitude on long westerly voyages uncovered new domains of scientific knowledge. One of these, though it proved to be a false trail from the navigator's viewpoint, was a new impetus to study magnetic attraction. In Columbus' time knowledge of magnetic attraction was by no means new in Europe. The power of an iron ore found near Magnesia in Asia to attract particles of iron had been widely known at least from the time of Thales (600 B.C.), the Greek master mariner whose successors regarded him as the founding father of geometry. It is possible that Greek-speaking navigators before the Christian era knew that a *lodestone* (the name given to a piece of such ore) will point in a particular direction when placed on a floating slab of cork or wood: but we have no records of such a device in Europe till about A.D. 1000, although we know that the Chinese were using one as a *south-pointing* compass long before that date. Magnetic compasses were being sold in the larger seaports when Columbus set out on his first voyage, and by then the makers had learned how to induce the attractive power of a suitably pointed fragment of ordinary iron by rubbing it with the natural magnetic ore.

However, it would be a mistake to assume that the mariner's compass freed the navigator from dependence on astronomical observations. The fact is that the compass needle points due north in very few places, and its precise direction varies in different parts of the world within limits of 50° east or west of the polar axis (Fig. 32). Columbus himself contributed to knowledge of how magnetic declination (i.e. deviation from the true north in the horizontal plane) varies from place to place, when he brought back observations on it from his voyages, as did his successors who circumnavigated the globe before the

31. *The Port of Lisbon at the time when the Portuguese were trading with the Far East and colonising the New World.*

end of the following century. In his famous treatise *Voyages of Elizabethan Seamen*, Hakluyt cites explicit instructions that sea captains of the Virgin Queen should record such variations. She herself was the patron and patient of William Gilbert, the physician who first made

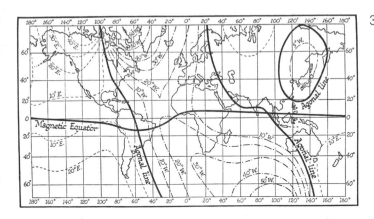

32. *Map showing the magnetic equator, where the dip is zero, and dotted lines where the deviation of the compass needle from the true north is the same. The* Agonal *lines go through places where the needle points due north.*

magnetism a matter of scientific experimentation (Fig. 34).

Studies of the earth's magnetic field in the sixteenth century led to the recognition of a new phenomenon, the *dip* (Fig. 33). The dip is the inclination of the magnetic needle to the plumb line when free to move in a vertical plane. By the end of the sixteenth century, many observations of the dip in different latitudes were available. Hudson, the explorer who gave his name to Hudson Bay, found that the needle in his time was vertical at a particular locality on latitude 75°N.

33. *Dipping needle.*

If we exclude casual references, the literature of magnetism starts with the observations of a Port of London compass-maker named Norman. In 1581, he published a book called *The New Attractive*. It is noteworthy chiefly because it broke away from fanciful notions which located the point of attraction in the Great Bear or, likewise irrelevantly, elsewhere. Norman asserted that the power to force the float to take up its characteristic horizontal position and the dipping needle to diverge from the vertical resides in the earth itself. William Gilbert, whose experiments on magnetism delighted the most cultivated (and virginal) monarch who ever occupied the English throne (Fig. 34), gave the experimental proof of this in his book *De Magnete*.

This treatise, published in 1600, is unique because it cites the earliest recorded example of the construction of a small-scale model to establish a large-scale physical hypothesis. Gilbert contrived the construction (Fig. 35) of a sphere of magnetic iron sufficiently large to make it possible to move over its surface both a horizontally and a vertically posed magnetic needle. With these, he mapped out from pole to pole his *terella* (small earth) into great circles of equal magnetic declination and small circles of equal dip parallel to the equator. It was therefore con-

34. *Gilbert demonstrating his experiments to Queen Elizabeth I.*

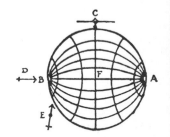

35. *Gilbert's* Terella, *a model for terrestrial magnetism.*

ceivable that combined use of magnetic declination and dip could replace astronomical observations as a means of locating a ship's position in two dimensions. Seemingly, the possibility was attractive to Elizabeth's sea captains. If so, it was probably because they were less adept astronomers than their Spanish competitors. The forlorn hope that construction of maps on a grid of intersecting lines of equivalent magnetic declination and of equivalent magnetic dip (Fig. 32) dogged British navigation for the better part of a century after Gilbert's time.

In 1676 one writer, Henry Bond, published a book *The Longitude Found*. Two years later another writer, Peter Blackbarrow, returned to the fray with the publication of *The Longitude Not Found*. In the interests of the Navy, during the closing years of the same century, the British Government solicited the co-operation of the Royal Society to construct a world chart of magnetic readings. When the report of its findings was completed in 1700, under the direction of Halley of comet fame, what extinguished hope was a fact which Flemish manufacturers of compasses already knew in Norman's time. Indeed, they forewarned their purchasers to that effect. The earth's magnetic field is not very stable, and map grids of the sort mentioned above must call for frequent revision. For instance, the deviation of the compass pointer from the true North at London has had the following values over a period including the defeat of the Spanish Armada and the suppression of nascent Spanish civilisation by Franco's Moroccan mercenaries:

1580	$11\frac{1}{4}°$E	1800	$24°$W
1665	$1\frac{1}{2}°$E	1925	$13\frac{1}{6}°$W
1765	$20°$W	1935	$11\frac{1}{2}°$W

When Gemma Frisius (p. 31) made the suggestion of using a sufficiently reliable clock to determine terrestrial longitude by the standard time of transit of a heavenly body, no clocks then available could keep time faithfully enough to realise this anticipation—nor indeed was one available till two hundred years later. However, even a Nuremberg Egg was preferable to an hour glass, if one's intention was to compare local time of an eclipse with the time forecast at a standard longitude, e.g. that of Nuremberg or Madrid.

Early clocks and watches were unreliable because their *escapement* was for one reason or another defective. An escapement (Fig. 36) is a device to make the driving wheel rotate as best it can through equal arcs in equal intervals of time. Common to different types is a bar with two arms so placed that when one engages a cog or tooth of the driving wheel, the other is free. It must thus swing to and fro engaging and freeing successive cogs or teeth. The earliest weight-driven clock had a so-called *verge* escape-

36. *Verge escapement etc. for earliest weight driven clocks.*

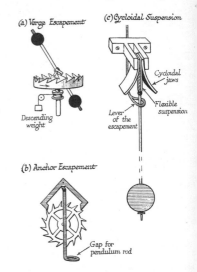

ment (Fig. 36) made to swing to and fro by a bar with a heavy ball at each end. The time interval of the swing in either direction was not very constant and the spacing of the cogs of the driving wheel was far from perfect. In later clocks and watches, the pendulum or the hairspring kept the escapement in motion.

The need of the navigator for an instrument sufficiently reliable to keep time throughout a long sea voyage gave a powerful drive to the clock and watch industry from the time of Frisius till the middle of the eighteenth century.

Meanwhile, there was urgent need for making better long-range forecasts of celestial signals. How this came to fruition will be the subject of our next chapter.

The end of the quest for what Newton's contemporaries called a seaworthy clock, and what we now call a *chronometer*, does not belong to the period with which this book deals. Still, it may satisfy the curiosity of the reader, if this chapter includes a brief recital of the story. Even if the workmanship of spacing the cogs on the wheels was above reproach, neither clocks nor watches of the sixteenth century had reliable regulators. Galileo's discovery (p. 87) that the period of the pendulum is very nearly constant for small angles encouraged hopes which seemed all the more justifiable when Huyghens showed that the constancy is exact, if the suspension forces the pendulum to swing in a cycloidal (Fig. 36) instead of a circular arc. How this hope proved to be an illusion, the reader will learn later (pp. 89–91).

A pendulum regulator is useless for a watch and it is doubtful whether a pendulum clock could have been adaptable to very rough seas. Within two decades of the date when Galileo became a prisoner of the Inquisition, Hooke had invented in England the hairspring wheel regulator (Fig. 37) which our watches still have. In his time, little was known about the expansion of metals by heat, and experience soon proved that the original design did not pass the test of exposure to widely different temperatures at different latitudes. In desperation for its disappointment over the possible usefulness of the Mariner's Compass, the British Navy got its government to create out of public funds a *Board of Longitude* founded in 1714. The Act which inaugurated the Board assigned for payment of a reward of £20,000 for any method to enable a ship to establish its longitude with an error not ex-

D

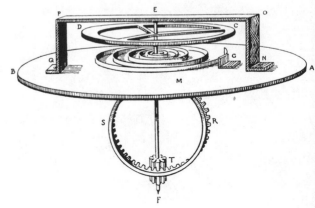

37. *Spring wheel watch regulator.*

38. *Huyghen's Clock with pendulum swing in a cycloidal arc to ensure absolute equality of the period.*

ceeding 30 miles at the end of a voyage to the West Indies.

In 1736, a Yorkshire carpenter named Harrison hit on the idea of making a balance wheel having concentric rims of two metals (brass and steel) with different temperature coefficients of expansion to ensure equal tension of the hairspring (Fig. 39). In what later became the flagship of Anson, an admiral who circumnavigated the globe, a test on a six week voyage to Lisbon led in the same year to a highly encouraging official report. This disclosed that Harrison located the Lizard on the coast of Cornwall, when the official navigator believed that he had reached a location "one degree and twenty-six miles east of it". Harrison did not submit this model for the £20,000

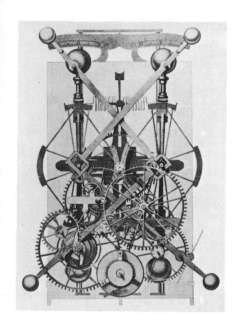

39. *Harrison's second
Chronometer model.*

reward. With small subsidies from the Board of Longitude, he persevered for twenty more years. His fourth model on a test voyage to Jamaica in 1761 incurred an error of only one mile; and the error was under ten miles in a voyage to Barbados three years later.

The Board was parsimonious about disposal of the promised prize. Harrison received half of it in 1765 and the other half eight years later, after a long quibble which was less lucrative to him than to his lawyers. Our history does not record precisely how little of the reward went to Harrison when his lawyers had taken their rake-off. For the use of Captain Cook, the Admiralty made an exact replica of the fourth model at a cost of £450.

4 **The Copernican Revolution**

More than once in previous chapters the reader has met the term *nautical almanacs*. It now means tables of astronomical data, tides and other information essential to scientific navigation. The name for compilations of astronomical data in mediaeval times was *ephemerides*. They already had a market having no connection with seafaring. In the fifteenth and sixteenth centuries the monarchs of Europe, the merchant princes and even the great banking corporations leaned heavily on, and paid handsomely for, the advice of astrologers. Among the astronomers of antiquity, we know of only one who repudiated their claims.

From the dawn of science, superstitions about heavenly portents no less than the social necessity of regulating the calendar and the demands of navigation had provided a sustained impetus to astronomical study. By their power to forecast eclipses as events of good or ill omen, the priestly astronomers of the temple had exploited the credulity of the laity to their own aggrandisement; and the temples of Iraq transmitted to posterity an elaborate body of doctrine concerning the influence exerted at birth by the planets on the future of the individual. For instance, in what sign of the zodiac were each of the planets at a person's birth had supposedly at that time a decisive effect on his or her worldly prospects, health and long life. In making such a prediction—casting a horoscope—there were other events at birth to which the astrologer attached importance, such as whether one or other of the planets happened to be in conjunction with the earth or the moon (p. 33).

For the reader who has not read the preceding instalment of *The Beginnings of Science*,* a digression may here be

Maps, Mirrors and Mechanics.

necessary to explain the meaning of some terms used in what follows. Since Ptolemy's time, astronomers have recognised two ways of locating a celestial body in space. Each conceives them as occupying a unique position in a hypothetical sphere—the Celestial Sphere—divided equally in two by a circular plane with an axis piercing its centre at right angles. In one system (Fig. 44), now used exclusively in maritime or aerial navigation, this plane includes that of the earth's equator, and one imagines the sphere to be lined up like a terrestrial globe with great circles passing through the earth's North and South Poles, and other circles parallel with the Celestial Equator. In the other system (Fig. 45), the lay-out of circles of both sorts is similar, but the plane which bisects the sphere is that of the *Ecliptic*, i.e. that in which the sun's apparent annual retreat occurs or—if we take the Copernican view —that in which the earth moves around the sun.

In the first system, one calls the great circles which are in the same planes as corresponding terrestrial meridians of longitude circles of *Right Ascension* (*R.A.*) and one speaks of those in the plane of corresponding circles of terrestrial latitude, as circles of *Declination*. The terms *celestial longitude* and *celestial latitude* refer to the system in which the plane of the ecliptic and its axis define the lay-out. This is very confusing, the more so because the calculation of celestial longitude and celestial latitude is immensely more complicated than the determination of R.A. and declination.

To determine R.A. and declination of a heavenly body, it suffices to observe the local time of its transit* and the angle it then makes (its meridian *zenith distance*) with the plumb line. The relation between declination, z.d. and

---

*i.e. when it reaches its highest point above the horizon plane.

the terrestrial latitude of the observer then follows from a geometrical construction well within the reach of a fourteen-year-old child of normal intelligence. The calculation of R.A., as for terrestrial longitude, depends only on the time interval between transits of heavenly bodies on different meridians. When reckoning our terrestrial longitude, this presupposes a standard meridian, now taken to be that on which the Greenwich observatory lies. The Greenwich of the Celestial Sphere in both systems, represented by ♈, is the point where the Ecliptic cuts the Equator at the Spring Equinox, i.e. at some time on March 21.

After the chronometer made it possible for the navigator to dispense with celestial signals and printing had made possible at little cost the periodical revision of tables showing the R.A. and Declination of any bright stars, there was no reason for complicating the determination of terrestrial latitude and longitude at sea by using tables based on an alternative system. The reader may therefore wonder why Ptolemy compiled them in this way. There were, in fact, two good reasons.

Owing to the very slow rotation (so-called *Precession of the Equinoxes*) of the plane of the ecliptic round that of the celestial equator, the position of the stars is not as fixed as the term implies. A complete cycle in which the R.A. of a star changes through 360° takes about 25,000 years. Meanwhile, its declination also changes. Both annual rates of change are very small, less than a hundredth of a degree, but some at least would be detectable by the instruments available in Ptolemy's time (i.e. about A.D. 140) after comparatively few years, and tables prepared several years earlier would be out of date. At a time when the speed of their distribution depended on the slow process of copying by hand, this consideration may well have influenced Ptolemy's choice. For the celestial latitude of a fixed star is not affected by the Precession of the Equinoxes, and the celestial longitude of all stars changes at the same steady annual rate. Given the date at which the table of the two was compiled, the user could make this trivial adjustment.

Because nearly all astronomers in Ptolemy's time were astrologers at heart and, as such, preoccupied with the position of the planets at birth, another consideration probably weighed with him. The orbits of the planets— at least of those then known—lie much closer to the ecliptic plane than to that of the celestial equator. Further-more, the sun's apparent motion in longitude is predict-able without recourse to tables; but the R.A. of the sun does not change steadily throughout the year like its celestial longitude. The latter increases at an almost exactly constant rate, slightly less than $1°$ per day.

The printing press, which already had a guaranteed market for ephemerides, made available to navigators data they could manipulate for a purpose other than the intention of those who first compiled or used them. Astrological superstition alone explains why the location of the planets occupies so prominent a position in early tabulations, and why those who compiled the first printed ephemeris undertook so formidable a task as describing their motions on the assumption that the earth is the centre of the universe. When Columbus returned from the New World in 1493, time was therefore ripe for a new and simpler recipe for making long range forecasts of planetary entries in the ephemerides. Fifty years later the recipe became available in printed form, when the Polish astronomer Copernicus published his *De Revolutionibus*

*Orbium Coelestium.** Before we study the new system, let us recall some of the visible vagaries of planetary motion.

Even before the astronomers of remote antiquity began to measure the motions of the heavenly bodies, two of the planets, Venus and Jupiter, must have impressed the sky-watcher with the exceptional brightness of their steady glow. The priestly astronomers of the pre-Columbian New World civilisations of Central America bestowed as minute attention on the Venus cycle as on their solar calendar. They built into their ritual a period of approximately 584 days, this being the interval between successive occasions when Venus has the same longitude as the sun, being nearest the earth, or the same longitude as the sun being furthest from it. The exact length of the Venus cycle is 583.92 days. To correct the error in taking it as 584 in a normal cycle, the Mayas introduced a 580 day cycle at the end of every sixty-one normal ones.

At a very early date, the temple astronomers of our earliest Old World civilisation could distinguish two sorts of planets. Venus, brighter than any star, even Sirius, and its much smaller sister Mercury, they learned to recognise only as morning stars rising just before dawn or as evening stars setting soon after sundown. In short, one sees neither of them at midnight and never at transit. We now call these two *inferior* planets (Fig. 42). Jupiter with Mars, less bright but commanding attention by its ruddy glow, we call by contrast *superior* planets (Fig. 43). They may be visible at times throughout the whole night.

What the inferior and superior planets have in common is that their rising and setting positions on the local

*As is true of so many European scholars as late as Linnaeus in the eighteenth century, Copernicus, a Pole, Latinised his native name (Nicolaus Koppernick). The English equivalent of the book's title is *Concerning the Revolutions of the Heavenly Bodies*. It went to the press in 1540 but a first draft had been circulated in manuscript among his friends ten years earlier.

horizon are not fixed as are those of the stars, at least to the naked eye throughout the course of a century. Sometimes their rising or setting positions drift northwards or southwards when those of the sun do the same. At other times, they change in the direction opposite to those of the sun. These vagaries earned them the name planet from the Greek word for a *wanderer*.

When more precise measurements on their hourly and daily co-ordinates with reference to the horizon plane accumulated, more especially through the work of Alexandrian astronomers in the three centuries B.C., it thus appeared that they sometimes seem to be moving in the sky in one direction, sometimes in the opposite. Both the existence of the two categories (*inferior* and *superior*) and the apparent reversal of their track in the heavens are easy to envisage (Fig. 41), if we are open to conviction that the earth is a planet, and like other planets revolves round the sun. We can then conceive that Venus and Mercury have orbits between the earth and the sun. Contrariwise, the earth's orbit is nearer to the sun than those of Mars, Jupiter and Saturn. This explains how some planets are, and others are never, visible at transit. If we conceive that the speed with which different planets move in their orbits differs from that of the earth in its own, we have also an explanation of *direct* and *retrograde* motion, i.e. why (as when on the side of the sun opposite to the earth) they appear to be moving one way and (when on the same side of the sun as the earth) they appear to move in opposite directions relative to ourselves.

Doubtless, such considerations led the astronomer Aristarchus, who flourished about 270 B.C., to favour the foregoing *heliocentric*, i.e. sun-centred, view in opposition to the then orthodox *geocentric* view, which places the earth at the centre of the universe and postulates that all

40. The Solar System of Ptolemy
In this system, there were 4 classes of motion here shown: (i) the daily rotation from east to west of the celestial sphere embracing all the heavenly bodies. As here drawn Venus and Mars are as when morning stars, (ii) the daily retreat from west and east of the moon in its monthly cycle and the sun in its annual cycle; (iii) two independent motions of the planets, one in an orbit round the earth in the same direction as (ii) above and one epicycle about a point on the orbit itself in the opposite direction to (ii). Our figure does not show two other motions of Ptolemy's system—the roughly 18-year cycle of the moon's nodes and the corresponding roughly 26,000-year solar cycle called the Precession of the Equinoxes.

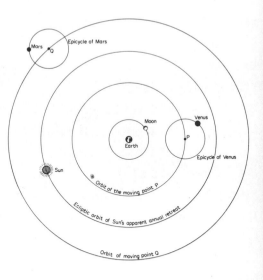

the heavenly bodies revolve, as does the moon, round it. Though the apparent daily motion of the sun and the apparent nightly motions of the other heavenly bodies are equally explicable on the assumption that the earth

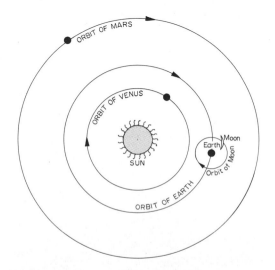

41. The Copernican System
Aside from the rotation of the Moon's nodes and the Precession of the Equinoxes, the Copernican Solar system recognised only three sorts of motion:
(i) the daily rotation of the earth from west to east.
(ii) the monthly cycle of the moon around the earth and annual cycle of the earth from east to west around the sun.
(iii) the orbits of the planets revolving around the sun in the same direction as the earth.
This figure shows only two planets one inferior (Venus), the other superior (Mars).

rotates on its axis, there were then no known facts to support this possibility which demands a greater effort of imagination than its alternative. Ptolemy rejected it for a reason which was compelling at a time when there was no means of measuring our distance from even the nearest of the fixed stars.

For schematising the apparent motions of the fixed stars in the absence of such knowledge, the geocentric view is simpler than its alternative. Indeed, current manuals for navigation by the fixed stars by night and the sun by day continue to adopt it, as if Copernicus had never existed. On the other hand it demands far greater effort of imagination to account for the antics of the planets if we do adopt it, and the mathematical difficulties of making forecasts of even tolerable reliability over long sea voyages are still, and were even more so in Newton's time, very formidable.

The general idea of the system which Ptolemy bequeathed to the technology of navigation on the threshold of the Columbian era had its origin in the speculations of Eudoxus, a Greek astronomer, about 300 B.C. If we confine such speculations to the *day-to-day*, in contradistinction to the *daily*, changes it set out to explain, Ptolemy's system assumed that each planet behaved as if it had two concurrent motions, an orbital and an epicyclic (Fig. 41). The epicycle was a circular revolution about a point moving in its orbital track with the earth as centre. In Ptolemaic astronomy, the orbits of these moving points were smaller than that of the sun in the case of Venus and Mercury, but larger in the case of Mars, Jupiter and Saturn. Beyond the outermost planetary orbits of this system was a great sphere on which lie the fixed stars.

Few, if any, readers of this book would be able to follow the procedure of making a short term planetary forecast with tolerable reliability by mathematical manipulation of the epicycles. In any case, the exercise would be of historic interest only. On the other hand, it should not be too difficult for the reader to understand how the Copernican world view enables us to forecast a planet's position on the assumption—that of Copernicus himself—that it moves in a *circular* orbit round the sun. Actually, as Kepler showed at a later date, they move in elliptical orbits. However, an ellipse merges into a circle when any axis (i.e. a straight line through the centre to the boundary) is equal to any other. If therefore the ratio of the shortest to the longest axis of an ellipse differs only slightly from unity, the figure is very nearly circular. This is true of the orbits of Venus and Mars. For Venus its value correct to 6 decimal figures is 0.999976. For Mars its value is 0.995666.

To solve the problem of how to make a Copernican forecast where a planet will later be from our knowledge of its position relative to the earth on a particular day, we need to know two things: (a) the spacing of the orbits of planet and earth *relative* to the sun; (b) the time it takes the planet to complete one revolution in its orbit. For each of these exercises we shall need to make different prescriptions for an inferior and a superior planet. Since both have orbits so nearly circular, our exhibits for the defence will be Venus (*inferior*) and Mars (*superior*).

Let us therefore start by learning how to make a scale diagram showing the *relative* (not absolute) distances of the earth and Venus from the sun. In this case, the line joining the earth to the points on the orbit of Venus where it is first visible as a morning star (or is last visible as an evening star) is tangential to it. In our figure (Fig. 42) the line E ♈ is the Greenwich meridian of the Celestial Sphere. Since we are making a scale diagram, the radius of the earth's orbit (SE) may be of any suitable length. We can

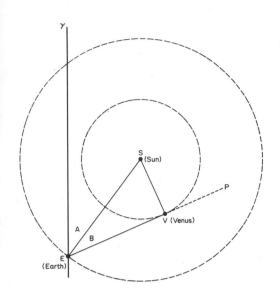

42. Orbit of Venus.

determine the angles A and B by observation, since A is then the sun's longitude and B is the difference between the longitude of Venus and that of the sun. Thus we can fill in *ES* the line on which *V* lies. Since the line joining *E* to *V* is tangent to the orbit of Venus at so-called *greatest elongation*, i.e. when about to disappear (or reappear) in the course of its circuit, we must complete the triangle *ESV* so that the angle *EVS* is a right angle. We now describe a circle with radius *SV* and *S* as centre. This will represent the orbit of Venus. We then see that:

$$\frac{\text{distance of Venus from the sun}}{\text{distance of Earth from the sun}} = \frac{SV}{SE}$$

In the language of trigonometry $SV \div SE = \sin B$, so that

$$\frac{\text{distance of Venus from the sun}}{\text{distance of Earth from the sun}} = \frac{\sin (\text{longit. of Venus}}{\textit{minus} \text{ longit. of Sun})}$$

To make a scale diagram showing the relative distances of Mars and Earth from the sun confronts us with a different problem. If Venus and the earth are in line with the sun when Venus is nearest the earth, the sun will be facing its illuminated surface and Venus will never transit visibly at midnight. Being a superior planet, Mars can do

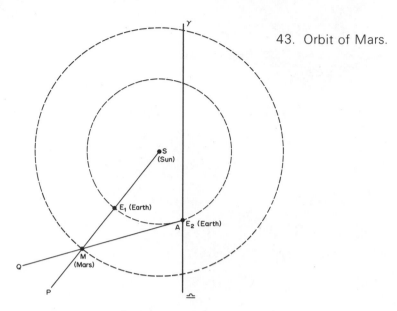

43. Orbit of Mars.

so. We can thus consider a situation (Fig. 43) in which Mars transits at midnight when its longitude is by observation that of the sun, i.e. when Mars (M), the earth (at E_1) and the sun are on the same meridian SE_1P. We can now suppose that Mars completes a revolution in its orbit, so that it is again in the same position, i.e. somewhere along the line SP after an interval of D days. Since we know that the earth completes its revolution in $365\frac{1}{4}$ days, gaining in longitude therefore $(360 \div 365\frac{1}{4})$ degrees per day, we can locate the earth's position (E_2) on our scale map if we know how to determine D as shown below. On our scale diagram M now lies on a line E_2Q which we can locate as follows. It makes an angle A with the line shown as passing through ♈ and a point 180° beyond ♈. So the longitude of Mars when the earth is at E_2 is $A + 180°$. We can now fill in E_2Q from observation of the longitude of Mars on that date. Since M also lies on the line E_1P, M lies at the point where E_1P and E_2Q intersect, and a radius of the orbit of Mars is the line SM. Thus we derive:

$$\frac{\text{distance of Earth from Sun}}{\text{distance of Mars from Sun}} = \frac{SE_1}{SM}$$

Suppose Venus takes V days to complete its orbit round

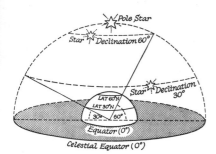 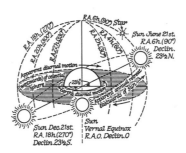

44. *Declination and Right Ascension.*
On the left: *two stars, one a zenith star at terrestrial latitude 30°, the other a zenith star at terrestrial latitude 60°.*
On the right: *A star whose R.A. is 6 hours transits almost exactly six hours after noon on the spring equinox.*

the sun, whence $(360 \div V)$ degrees per day, while the earth gains approximately $(360 \div 365)$ degrees per day. Relative to the earth which moves more slowly it has gained only:

$$\frac{360}{V} - \frac{360}{365}$$

From direct observation, the time taken for Venus to regain its same position relative to the earth, i.e. the interval between two successive occasions when the celestial longitudes of the two are identical, is approximately 584 days. So relative to the earth, Venus gains $(360 \div 584)$ degrees per day, so that (approximately):

$$\frac{360}{584} = \frac{360}{V} - \frac{360}{365} \quad and \quad \frac{1}{V} = \frac{1}{584} + \frac{1}{365}$$

This yields $V = 225$. If we use more precise values (583.92 and 365.25) for the Venus cycle and for the year, we derive as the time taken by Venus to complete its orbit (its *sidereal* period), 224.7 days.

If we now use M for the sidereal period of Mars, which completes a cycle between two conjunctions in approximately 766 days, the calculation is not the same, since we assume (as results justify) that the superior planets revolve more slowly than the earth. The earth then gains on the planet. Relative to the earth, the planet therefore gains approximately in degrees per day:

$$\frac{360}{365} - \frac{360}{766} \quad and \quad \frac{1}{M} = \frac{1}{365} - \frac{1}{766}$$

Using more precise values than 365 and 766, we obtain for the sidereal period of Mars 686.98 days.

What these figures add up to is that Venus gains in celestial longitude (to the nearest digit) $(360 \div 225)$ degrees per day and Mars gains $(360 \div 687)$ degrees per day. If then we know the longitude of earth and planet on any one day, we can place both in their relative positions on our Copernican scale diagrams D days later. In other words, we have solved the problem of how to make a forecast. We have a new recipe for such entries in our ephemerides as a date and hour when Venus will cease to be an evening, or first appear as a morning, star.

45. *Two methods of Mapping Celestial Bodies.*

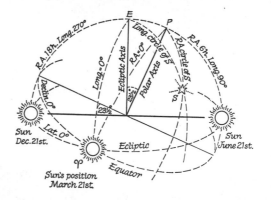

Both practical mathematics and astronomy profited from its impact when the printing press made available the work of Copernicus. It might have been a private communication to his friends had not his younger professorial colleague, Rheticus, seen it through the press during the three years before its ailing author died. Rheticus (his Latin *nom de plume* for Georg Joachim) issued with it an accompanying treatise on the trigonometrical calculations involved. Until his death in 1576, he continued the preparation, published twenty years later, of tables of sines, cosines, tangents, etc. for every one-sixtieth of a degree to ten decimal places. Such was the prelude to the discovery (somewhat obscurely) of logarithms by Napier in Scotland (1614). The issue of the first tables of logarithms by Briggs in England (1617) as an aid to computation occurred shortly after invention of the telescope had given a new impetus to precision of astronomical observation.

Ephemerides based on the Copernican theory, which still clung to the Greek tradition that only the circle (being the perfect plane figure) befits the proper respect we owe to the heavenly bodies, were not merely more reliable than their predecessors. What was equally important was that it involved far less effort to compile them as recipes for forecasts of planetary motions. This gave an impetus to more precise mapping of them. The man who made the greatest contribution before the turn of the century was the Danish astronomer, Tycho Brahe. Equipped in 1571 with an observatory in the castle of a patron, his maternal uncle, he received from the Danish Crown a better observatory, as a reward for discovery of a new star. Later, the occupant of the imperial throne of the residual Holy Roman Empire assigned him another castle and a still better observatory in Prague, two years before his death in 1601.

Kepler joined him as a pupil during the previous year. Then twenty-three years old, appointed in 1594 a professor of science in Graz, he was already familiar with the Copernican viewpoint. Since his first duties demanded a knowledge of astrological lore (a belief in which he never fully outgrew), Kepler set himself to master the underlying principles as laid down for the Ptolemaic system. Happily

E

for posterity, if not for domesticity, he married a wealthy German heiress capable of keeping him in a state to which he was not as yet accustomed and of keeping his name before the establishment. Appointed successor to Tycho Brahe as imperial mathematician at Prague, his first works dealt with astrology to the taste of his Imperial Highness. He drew the horoscopes of the Emperor and of other top persons, including the Military Chief of Staff, Wallenstein, and dedicated to the Emperor a treatise on the "great conjunction" of that year (1603).

Though this recital throws no light on the case for or against Copernicus, it is worthy of record, lest we forget that great scientific innovators may entertain very improbable views. Napier of logarithm fame nearly failed to complete the work that made him famous because he was determined to demonstrate by number magic from Holy Writ that the number of the Beast in the Apocalypse identified it with the ruling Pope. Newton spent much of his leisure from his duties at the Mint in old age interpreting the prophecies of the Book of Daniel. Comparable contemporary celebrities of the scientific scene are not far to seek.

However, Kepler took his job as a scientist sufficiently seriously to make a study of optics with a view to establishing—unsuccessfully—a general law of refraction in its bearing on astronomy (1604). He was prompt to enlist (1611) the telescope to refine astronomical observation. Before that he had already established the three laws named after him. Briefly these amount to two assertions in modern terms. *First*, the orbits of the planets are ellipses, albeit some (especially that of Venus) are very nearly circular. *Second*, their accelerations towards the sun are inversely proportional to the square of the distances which separate it from them.

This second law, which is the springboard from which Newton's theory of universal gravitation made a great leap forward half a century later, does not come within the scope of *The Beginnings of Science*. The first, however, does. On the basis of this emendation of the Copernican interpretation, Kepler published one of a reformed series of ephemerides in 1617. This was the year in which Briggs published his first tables of logarithms. Kepler availed himself immediately of so useful a means of reducing the labour of computation. In the forefront among astronomers to take advantage of them, he dedicated to Napier in 1620 an ephemeris computed with the aid of logarithms, and he did much to publicise them in Germany by a treatise published (1624) in the same year as a new table of Briggs citing logarithms of 30,000 natural numbers to 14 significant figures with corresponding logarithmic sines, cosines and tangents to 15 places for the hundredth part of every degree.

Kepler spent the rest of his working life issuing new ephemerides and tables of refraction. He also edited a catalogue of 777 stars compiled by Tycho Brahe. His final ephemerides, which made forecasts up to six years after his death in 1630, included two which are memorable. One, the transit of Mercury across the sun's disc, occurred the following year. No transit of a planet across the sun had hitherto been seen. Gassendi (p. 91) observed it in Paris on November 7, 1631. That of Venus for December 6 following was unfortunately invisible in Western Europe.

5 **From Spectacles to Satellites**

Early in the story of the Alexandrian episode, that is to say nearly three centuries before the beginning of the Christian era, the geometrical representation of a beam of light in terms of rays, i.e. straight lines, had bequeathed to posterity a correct account of the laws of reflection for plane, concave and convex mirrors. During the first two centuries A.D., Ptolemy and other astronomers among his contemporaries made experiments on the refraction of light. Their end in view was to correct for the apparent time of sunrise or sunset owing to the bending of light rays on entry into the earth's atmosphere. Magnification by lenses was still in the womb of time.

There is here no need to repeat the story (pp. 21–2) of how spectacles came into the picture two centuries before printing began, or why a craft of spectacle makers grew prosperous when elderly people (Fig. 22) became aware of the difficulties of reading small print. Nor do we need to recall how the innovation of perspective art by the great painters of the Italian Renaissance (A.D. 1300–1550) revived interest in the geometrical representation of light propagation. Somewhat oddly, the introduction of lenses did not immediately stimulate further enquiry into how light rays change their direction when they enter a new medium—as from outer space to our atmosphere or from air to water. Indeed, their use did not quicken interest from the level at which Ptolemy, and later Moorish physicians, left it till we reach the early years of the century in which the topic of this instalment of *The Beginnings of Science* ends.

Very soon however, in the context of now available and relatively cheap transparent glass, the spectacle industry gave birth to two new tools, each with a powerful and lasting influence on the progress of science. The name *telescope* bestowed by Galileo in 1612 was that of the

later one. In October, 1608, the assembly of the States
General at the Hague considered an application by Hans
Lippershey, a spectacle-maker, and voted later in the year
900 florins for his invention for seeing at a distance. The
story goes that he discovered how to do so by noticing
that he could bring a neighbouring church spire into
closer view by holding two spectacles some distance
apart. Galileo tells us that he got wind of the device while
in Venice a year later. On his return to Padua, he made an
instrument (Fig. 46) by fixing, instead of two convex
lenses, a convex and a concave, one at each end of a
leaden tube. In 1620, he was the first human being
to see that the planet Jupiter has moons in orbit around it.

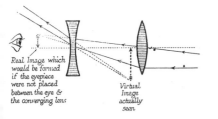

Real Image which
would be formed
if the eyepiece
were not placed
between the eye &
the converging lens

Virtual
Image
actually
seen

46. *Arrangement of
lenses in Galileo's
Telescope.*

The first of his telescopes magnified only 3 diameters. A
later one magnified 8, and eventually he constructed a
telescope with a magnification of 33 diameters. According
to Professor Bernal, Galileo received from the Italian
prince Leonardo Donato a stipend of 1000 ducats and a
professorship for life. In a letter to the same prince he
drew attention to the uses of the telescope—military,
naval and for navigation in general. From the same
source, we learn that he offered to the King of Spain in
1616 a recipe for determining longitude by recourse to
eclipses of Jupiter's satellites. The Spanish monarch was
unwilling to accept his terms—a grandeeship and a large
sum of money. So Galileo made a second offer to the
States General of Holland. In the first, he had extolled by

implication the benefits of monarchy. In the other, he appealed, but again without success, to democratic sentiment.

His proposal of a new method for determining longitude eventually came into its own, though not in Galileo's lifetime. At a time when most reliable methods depended on comparing local time of celestial signals such as eclipses with the forecast of the time of their occurrence at a standard meridian, the fact that Jupiter has moons of its own offered new opportunities for observing such signals. Thus Whitaker's Almanac records only two eclipses and no planetary occultations visible at Greenwich in the year 1936; but it discloses that there were no less than 56 appearances and disappearances of one or other of Jupiter's satellites. For one of these, Cassini prepared tables used by the French Navy from 1690 onwards. A by-product of the work on Jupiter's satellites was the discovery of an unforeseen delay of the timing of an eclipse, as forecast by Cassini's tables, when the planet is on the side of the sun opposite to the earth. This delay led the Danish astronomer Römer to the correct inference that the propagation of light is not instantaneous. His calculations (1676) on this assumption supplied our first figure for the speed of light; but they received little recognition till after his death in 1710.

For his own researches, Kepler constructed in 1611 a telescope (Fig. 47) of the earlier type made by Lippershey. Eight years later, he published his work on the motion of Mars (*De Motibus Stella Martis*) which finally convinced men of science that the heliocentric view of Copernicus (p. 51) was in principle correct. By substituting for the circular orbits of Copernicus elliptical paths for the planets, Kepler could forecast their positions with greater precision than heretofore—and indeed, with trivial emen-

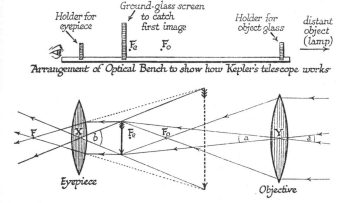

Holder for eyepiece | Ground-glass screen to catch first image | Holder for object glass | distant object (lamp)

F_e F_o

Arrangement of Optical Bench to show how Kepler's telescope works

F X b F_e F_o a Y a

Eyepiece   Objective

47. *Arrangement of lenses in Kepler's Telescope.*

dations, adequate to this day. To say that his contemporaries accepted the heliocentric view of planetary motion because it was factually correct would, however, be an overstatement. With what mathematics was available till the generation of Einstein, all one could say in its favour was that it provided a far more reliable basis for calculating where a planet would be visible at a given hour of the day on a given date than the Ptolemaic view could offer.

Meanwhile, the telescope had contributed to a new outlook in another way. By its means, Galileo had observed sun-spots, whence the motion of the sun on its own axis. By then, he had already seen that Jupiter had satellites which revolve around it as the moon revolves round the earth. So there were now other worlds than ours with satellites revolving round them; and if the sun could rotate on its axis, why not the earth? In short, his telescopic discoveries more than any other considerations led Galileo to give public support to the Copernican view. Contrary to scripture and to the teaching of Aristotle who shared equal authority with St Paul in mediaeval Catholic doctrine, this was still heresy. Indeed, his rejection of the geocentric view was one of the chief errors for which the Inquisition in 1600 had condemned the Italian scholar Giordano Bruno to death at the stake.

Aristotle's authority had never before been so indispensable a prop to priestly authority. While Protestant reformers pilloried the doctrine of transubstantiation, only Aristotle's unintelligible distinction between *essence* and *substance* could comfort the faithful. In 1611 Galileo visited Rome and exhibited to the Vatican the telescopic wonders of the heavens, including the mountains of the moon and stars of the Milky Way. Encouraged by the flattery of his reception, he published at Rome two years later his *Letters on the Solar Spots*, openly advocating the Copernican view. In 1616, the Inquisition issued a decree reaffirming that the heliocentric doctrine was heretical and the Pope—then Paul V—admonished Galileo to refrain from defending it.

As we shall see later, Galileo had already incurred the fury of the dominant party in the universities of Italy and France when he announced his discovery of terrestrial gravitation in contrariety to Aristotle's teaching. How firmly it was then entrenched, we may infer from an edict of the Parliament of Paris in 1610. This prohibited, under pain of death, the publication of any thesis without permission of the Faculty of the University of Paris. It was in this year that two Parisian chemists who disagreed with Aristotle about the number of elements (holding them to be five, not four) went to gaol, thence condemned to banishment after destruction of their publications. The year 1610 was the one in which Galileo discovered four of the satellites of Jupiter.

In what he judged to be the more liberal mental climate of 1632, Galileo published in Florence a treatise on the Copernican world view. It was received throughout Protestant Europe with acclamation, but its distribution was prohibited in Rome, where he was compelled to come before the Inquisition and to recant under threat of torture. The Holy Office then sentenced him to recite

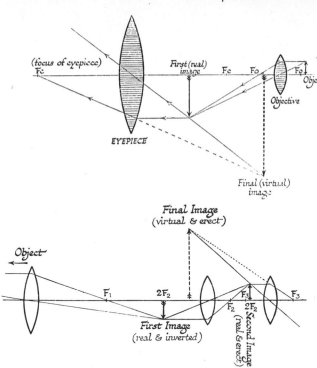

(focus of eyepiece) Fc — *First (real) image* Fc Fo — *Fo Object* — *Objective*

EYEPIECE

Final (virtual) image

Final Image (virtual & erect)

Object

F_1 $2F_2$ F_3 F_3
F_2 $2F_2$

First Image (real & inverted)

Second Image (real & erect)

48. *Image of a Telescope designed like this one is inverted, but an additional lens for the eyepiece can make it erect.*

once a week for three years the seven penitential psalms. History does not record whether he did so when allowed to return to his home in Florence six months later.

Doubtless, the teaching of Copernicus, as amended by Kepler, would have triumphed if the telescope had not been invented. On the other hand, vast tracts of biological science would have remained for ever unexplored if there had been no microscope. Wolf tells us that "the credit for the invention of the compound microscope", i.e. an arrangement of two lenses for magnifying near objects, is probably due to Zacharias Jensen, like Hans Lippershey a Dutch spectacle-maker. He "chanced on the invention by a happy accident about the year 1590". His instrument was a "combination of a double convex lens and a double concave lens". Galileo himself was one of the first to use one. Before he constructed a telescope, he had made observations *inter alia* on the compound eyes of insects.

We have seen that the response of astronomers to the possibilities of the newly invented telescope was well nigh instantaneous. So the reader might expect this chapter to record how biological science, now equipped with a new key to unlock so many of nature's secrets,

49. *An early Microscope. With this instrument, Hooke made the observations embodied in his* Micrographia *(1665) the first treatise wholly devoted to microscopic observations.*

could quickly advance on a wide front in the generation following the invention of the microscope. Nothing of the sort happened. For fifty years it remained a toy for amateurs with no prevision of its potential. Meanwhile, it could have been the means to solve conclusively problems long since crying aloud for solution. Strictly speaking therefore, the microscope does not come into its own in the story of how science began, as we shall leave it in this book at the death of Galileo in the same year as the birth of Newton (1642).

Its so belated benefits bequeath a challenge to curiosity; what problems had so long to await a convincing solution —and if so why? The work of William Harvey (1578–1657) illustrates two of this sort, and the more enigmatic because Harvey himself made little—if indeed any—use of what could have been for him so powerful a tool. Better known in connexion with the circulation of the blood, Harvey had to dispose of more than a millennium of teaching transmitted from Galen (about A.D. 180) through Moslem translations of Alexandrian treatises. According to the orthodoxy of his time, the blood circulates from the right to the left side of the heart (or *vice versa*) through minute pores in the septa between the ventricles. Microscopic examination of the septa could have speedily disposed of this delusion. Harvey maintained, correctly, that the heart works pump-wise in a closed circle from the right ventricle through the pulmonary artery to the lungs, thence from the pulmonary veins to the left auricle, from the left ventricle *via* the aorta to the rest of the body and thence by the caval veins back to the right auricle.

All this implied the existence of vessels between the visible ends of the arteries and the beginning of the veins, albeit too small to be seen with the naked eye. As every first-year medical student now knows, a single glance at the stretched web of the foot of a frog under the microscope would have sufficed to show Harvey both the existence of this missing link, i.e. the *capillaries*, and the continuous flow of the blood through them in one direction, as his teaching implied. It remained for Malpighi to see this for himself, and to record it, in 1660, thirty-two years after Harvey published his treatise on the circulation of the blood.

Of scarcely less importance in the history of biology is Harvey's work on reproduction, published in a treatise more than five times as long as that on the circulation, and published much later (in 1651). At that time, physicians and amateur naturalists had inherited from Aristotle's teaching the belief that many animals arise spontaneously from mud and rotten matter. Indeed, even more fantastic beliefs persisted thirty years later. One such is the goose barnacle legend which is worth quoting, as narrated at the end of Gerard's *Herbal* (1594), a botanical publication:

There is a small Island in Lancashire where are found the broken pieces of old and bruised ships . . . and also the trunks and bodies with the branches of old and rotten trees . . . whereon is found a certain spume or froth that in time breedeth unto certain shells in shape like those of the Muskle, wherein is contained a thing in form like lace or silk . . . one end of which is fastened unto the inside of the shell even as fish of Oisters and Muskles are: the other end is made fast unto the belly of a rude masse or lumpe which in time cometh to the shape of a bird; when it is perfectly formed, the shell gapeth open and the first thing that appeareth is the aforesaid lace or string; next come the legs of the bird hanging out and as it groweth greater it openeth the shell by degrees til at length it is all come forth and hangeth only by the bill: in short space after it cometh to full maturitie and falleth into the sea where it gathereth feathers and groweth to a fowle bigger than a Mallard and less than a goose having blacke legs and bill or beak and feathers blacke and white spotted in such manner as is our magpie . . . We conclude and end our present Volume with this Wonder of England. For the which God's name be ever honoured and praised.

Here follows a representative specimen from Aristotle's *Natural History*, dealing with reproduction of invertebrates:

Some of them are produced from similar animals, as phalangia and spiders from phalangia and spiders . . . others do not originate in animals of the same species but their reproduction is spontaneous, for some of them spring from the dew which falls from plants. Others originate in rotten mud and dung. Butterflies are produced from caterpillars and these originate in the leaves of green plants . . . The gnats originate in ascarides (*i.e. thread worms*) and the ascarides originate in the mud of wells and running waters that flow over an earthy bottom. At first, the decaying mud acquires a white colour which afterwards becomes black and finally red.

Against all such superstitions, Harvey asserted the principle that *like begets like* or, as in the English translation of a Latin quotation (*omnia vivum ex ovo*) from his treatise on reproduction: every living thing starts from an egg. To be sure, he registered a few reservations about some creatures whose ova are too small to be visible without magnification; but writing more than fifty years after the patent of Zacharias Jensen, he could have dis-

posed of any lingering doubts on that score with a microscope at his disposal.

This treatise on reproduction is the first of its kind on
embryology, including a realistic description of the
development of the hen's egg and of early mammalian
embryos as seen with the naked eye. It discredited not a
few superstitions such as spontaneous generation; but it
could have been vastly more informative and challenging
if the author had equipped himself with so powerful a
tool as the microscope, long since to hand. Meanwhile,
amateurs plodded on, content to identify organisms of
microscopic size beyond the ken of their predecessors—
as Stelluti states (1630) "to my no less joy than marvel,
since they are unknown to Aristotle and to any other
naturalist".

What then is the answer to the question raised earlier:
why did biological science so tardily learn to exploit the
use of the microscope? One of Oscar Wilde's characters,
when asked by someone to tell the truth pure and simple,
replies that truth is never pure and rarely simple. Indeed,
no simple explanation accounts for the belated welcome
to the invention of the microscope, a delay in sharp contrast to the way in which the telescope so speedily found
a market. However, it is a fact that scholarly astronomers
were by no means the only people to whom the telescope
was saleable. It was invaluable to the ship's pilot in search
of a recognisable coast. With it the commander of a naval
squadron could count the enemy's ships long before he
could do so with the naked eye. It was also very useful to
the officer in command of artillery as a means of assessing
more precisely than hitherto the range for reaching the
required target.

Contrariwise, the only potential consumers for the
lately invented microscope were wealthy dabblers in

natural history, or surgeons—both of whom had other preoccupations at the time. In the context of expanding navigation and exploration following the Columbian voyages, the astronomer had much to offer the patrons who financed him; but biology had at that time, as its patrons, only wealthy princes for whom zoological gardens were a coveted form of conspicuous expenditure, affluent merchants and nobles who employed their own physicians and the apothecary who derived his income largely from dispensing herbs of allegedly medicinal value.

In this set-up, exploration diverted much of the energy of scholars so disposed into cataloguing an ever increasing number of unfamiliar species of animals and plants; and medical teachers were still too intoxicated with the new freedom for dissection sponsored by the publication of the treatise of Vesalius (p. 12) to exploit the use of any instruments other than forceps, scissors and scalpel. In short, biological studies had in Harvey's time very little sales appeal, whence also little incentive to adventure.

That the scalpel, forceps and scissors maintained their supremacy after introduction of the microscope among physicians with wealthy patrons—Charles I being a patron and companion to Harvey—is less unintelligible, if one recalls how many crude errors of Galen anyone with dissecting instruments could expose, as for instance, did Fabricius, an Italian surgeon and one of Harvey's teachers, when he published in 1603 a monograph describing the discovery that veins (Fig. 50) have valves which keep the blood stream flowing in one direction when the ventricles of the heart prime the pump again.

Galen's own account of the blood flow was as follows. The liver endows the blood with its "natural spirits". Thence the blood flows through the veins to other parts,

50. On the left: *illustration from the treatise of Fabricius showing valves of a vein of the human leg.*
On the right: *diagrammatic view of three sets of valves in a vein.*

returning to its source by an ebb and flow movement like the tides. From the right ventricle it returns to the heart after discharging impurities into the lungs. Through pores in the septum between the ventricles after refinement of its vital spirits, it passes to the brain where it gets a purification by collecting animal spirits, and the nerves (conceived erroneously as tubes) distribute them throughout the body.

While such beliefs were acceptable, scalpel, scissors and forceps could pay dividends. Even so, Fabricius did not fully exploit their usefulness. Though he recorded how the valves swell up if a tourniquet obstructs the veinous flow, he was content to record the erroneous opinion that they retarded the flow of the blood to give the tissues time to digest the food they fed to it.

The impact on optical science of two such inventions as we have here discussed was comparatively prompt. Though the laws of reflection from curved surfaces were well established by Alexandrian pioneers, nothing comparable was known about formation of images by lenses till we reach the end of the period with which this book deals. What antiquity had bequeathed us about refraction was an empirical rule which was approximately true only for small angles of incidence involved in atmospheric refraction of light rays from remote celestial bodies. Kepler made an unsuccessful attempt to explain image formation by lenses in terms of what little he and his contemporariés knew of refraction; but the first person known to announce a correct rule—though he did not give it in the form we learn today—was a Dutchman, Snell, in 1621 (Fig. 51). From this, as every elementary text-book of physics explains, follow two rules which suffice to locate images, real or virtual, formed by thin lenses (Figs. 52 and 53):

(a) a ray does not change its direction in passing through the optical centre of a lens;

(b) rays parallel to the optical axis (i.e. a line passing through the centre and at right angles to the plane in which lie the edges of the lens) converge to (biconvex lens) or diverge from (biconcave lens) a single point (the *focus*).

51. *Snell's Law of Refraction.*

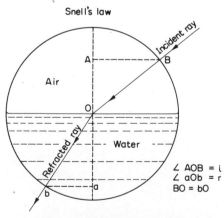

Snell's law

$\angle AOB = i$
$\angle aOb = r$
$BO = bO$

$\frac{AB}{ab} = \mu$ (a constant for any two media, e.g. air and water, called the *refractive index*)

$\frac{AB}{BO} = \sin i; \quad \frac{ab}{bO} = \sin r \quad \therefore \quad \frac{\sin i}{\sin r} = \mu$

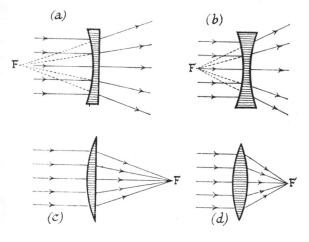

52. Above : *Diverging Lenses.*
     Below : *Converging Lenses.*

(a) (b) (c) (d)

53. *Formation of Images by Lenses.*

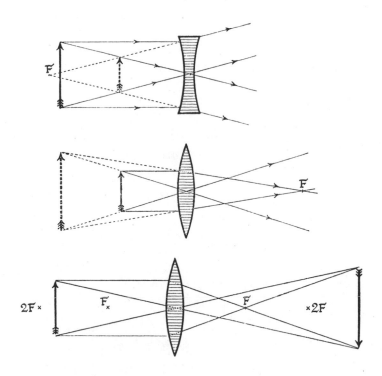

6 Track of the Cannon Ball and Swing of the Pendulum

We have seen in Chapter 2 that a characteristic feature of the phase of history dealt with in this instalment of *The Beginnings of Science* was a proliferation of inventions, partly a cause of and partly a result of new scientific discoveries. Such intensive inventive ingenuity brings into focus one way in which this period differs conspicuously from earlier times. There was now an upsurge of experimentation and with it, for the first time in the history of science, an intimate relation between the experimentalist and the mathematician.

In the forefront of sixteenth-century experimenters was Stevinus. Born sixteen years before Galileo, he was quartermaster in the army of William of Orange during the Dutch war of liberation. Stevinus added to general knowledge two new principles of equilibrium, each of which has a significant bearing on Galileo's discoveries about motion. The first of these is the condition of rest, i.e. the balance of two opposed motions, when one body hangs vertically downwards and a second heavier one rests on a smooth flat surface—so-called *inclined plane*—down which it would glide if not attached by a cord to the other (Figs. 54, 54A and 55). If we write m for the mass (p. 78) of a lighter one suspended vertically and M for that of a heavier one free to glide on the inclined plane, we may express the condition of equilibrium by the relation

$$\frac{m}{M} = \sin A$$

Of no less importance was the work of Stevinus on what was once called the *hydrostatic paradox*. This was the foundation for his proof that liquids exert by their weight at the same level equal pressure in every direction, in particular vertically upwards as well as downwards. Stevinus demonstrated that pressure exerted upwards by

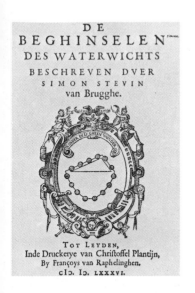

54. *Title page of a treatise by Stevinus displaying the figure on which he based his argument for the condition of equilibrium between weights resting on smooth surfaces inclined to one another and connected by a cord. The argument is as follows. A chain* longer than the two inclined planes is joined at its two ends and hangs from their common edge. If the two weights (masses) were not in equilibrium, they would be in perpetual motion. Since perpetual motion is an impossibility, they must be at rest (see Key in Figure 54A).

a liquid is equal to that due to the column above it by placing a metal plate (Fig. 56) over one of the open ends of a tube and plunging it vertically plate downwards into a bowl of water. He found that the plate did not fall off, as it would have done unless the liquid balanced the downward pressures on its edges by a force directed upwards. We shall see later that this discovery gave a new meaning to the principle of buoyancy discovered by Archimedes (Fig. 66). It also gave Galileo the clue to

54A. *Key to the diagram in Fig. 54.*
The line ab *is where two inclined planes with a common edge cut a horizontal plane. The argument illustrated in Fig. 54 presupposes that:*
(a) links of the chain are of equal mass and length, as is theoretically possible; *(b) the length of each sloping surface corresponds to an exact number of links, a condition rarely realisable. Accordingly, the law demands experimental proof.*

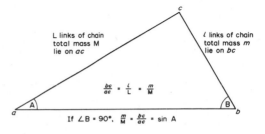

L links of chain
total mass M
lie on ac

l links of chain
total mass m
lie on bc

$$\frac{bc}{ac} = \frac{l}{L} = \frac{m}{M}$$

If $\angle B = 90°$, $\frac{m}{M} = \frac{bc}{ac} = \sin A$

55. *Experimental Proof of the Law of Equilibrium on an Inclined Plane. To tie up later with Galileo's Law of Motion on an inclined plane (Figs. 58 and 59), it will suffice if we assume that the smaller mass m hangs vertically and that the larger one (M) is free to move on a plane inclined to the horizontal at an angle A. In this illustration M and m each include the mass of the trolley and we assume that of the cord to be negligible.*

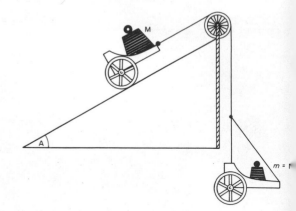

dispose of an objection to his theory of terrestrial gravitation.

The hydrostatic paradox is that the force exerted by a liquid on the bottom of a vessel depends only upon the area of the surface under pressure and the height of the liquid above it. In other words, the effect of the weight of water above a certain level depends only on the force it exerts per unit area. Force per unit area thus becomes our definition of *fluid pressure*, when we say that pressure in one direction is equal to pressure in another. Stevinus showed this (Fig. 57) by constructing two vessels of equal height having a round aperture at the bottom. The areas both of the aperture and of a disc which fitted over it in each vessel were equal; but the width of the column of fluid above one was much greater than that of the column above the other. To the centre of each disc he fixed a cord attached to the alternate limb of each balance, so that they filled either vessel with water, the weight of the column of water sufficed to make the discs seal the aperture below, so that no liquid escaped. He adjusted the weights attached to the alternate limb of each balance, so that they were in equilibrium with that of the force exerted by the equal columns of water above each disc. It turned out that the two weights were equal though the volumes of water

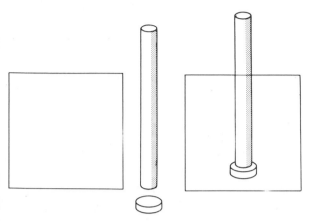

56. *Experiment to show that a liquid exerts the same upward and downward pressure at a given depth.*

above were very different. Only the height of the column of water and the area on which it exerted its effect contributed to the equilibrium between the force exerted by the liquid and the weight of the balance.

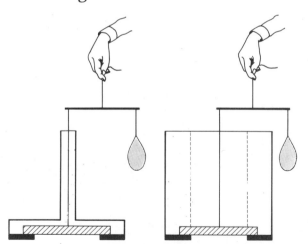

57. *Experiment to demonstrate the Hydrostatic Paradox. The aperture on the base of each vessel, the plate which closes it by the downward pressure of their liquid content, the heights of the liquid are equal. So also are the weights which balance the pressure on the two plates despite the fact that the volume of liquid pressing on them is very different.*

The work of Stevinus on fluid pressure established the principle of the hydraulic (Bramah) press, though he did not himself live to see its application as such. In mathematics he was one of the pioneers of algebraic symbolism and advocated legal adoption of decimal instead of vulgar fractions. In his military capacity to the Dutch forces of liberation, he devised a useful application of the formula for the sum of the squares of the first n natural numbers.

If one piles cannon balls in a pyramid, it is then necessary to count only the number of balls on an edge.

By 1600 Galileo, then a professor, first in the Italian university at Pisa and later at Padua, had laid the foundations of a new science of motion. Perhaps because astronomy engrossed his interest soon after that date, he did not publish his results in full until 1638. Before the turn of the preceding century, he had already angered his colleagues who mostly adhered to the Aristotelian doctrine of gravitation. According to Aristotle, the weight of solid bodies determines the speed they gain when they fall. Contrariwise, Galileo had shown that *heavy* bodies—i.e. as we should now say bodies immensely heavy in comparison with air—reach the ground simultaneously, if released together to fall from the same height. This led him to a correct interpretation of the path of the cannon ball.

To accomplish this outstanding contribution to the technology of his time, Galileo had to establish in quantitative terms how bodies fall under gravity. Watching them fall from a great height was then impracticable. The stopwatch was not as yet available and the time interval was too short for accurate observation by means then available. He therefore took advantage of the fact that one can slow down the motion of highly polished metal or wooden balls on highly polished sloping surfaces by diminishing the inclination of the latter to the horizontal plane. So he set out to establish for motion, as had Stevinus for rest, a quantitative law of the inclined plane (Figs. 58 and 59). Here we shall condense his argument by using the more compact language of algebra and trigonometry instead of the geometrical construction which Galileo used to interpret his data. In this situation, while the ball rolls through a distance d in a time interval t, we may write for the

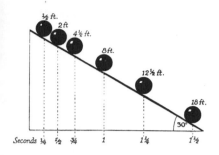

58. *Motion of a smooth ball on a smooth surface inclined at 30° to the horizontal base.*

59. *Motion of a smooth ball on a smooth inclined plane.*

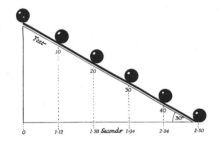

final velocity v, and since the initial velocity is zero, the mean velocity is $\frac{1}{2}(O + v) = \frac{1}{2}v$. If the acceleration a is constant, being the velocity gained in the same time t:

$$\frac{d}{t} = \frac{v}{2} \quad and \quad a = \frac{v}{t} \quad so \ that \quad a = \frac{2d}{t^2} \quad and \quad d = \frac{1}{2}at^2$$

To measure so short an interval as t, no wheel-driven clocks at that time were sufficiently sensitive. So Galileo fell back on a home-made clepsydra (waterclock)*, weighing the amount of water outflow as a measure of t. In this way he found that for different angles A_1 and A_2 of the inclination of planes of equal length (d), when tilted through vertical elevations p_1 and p_2 respectively, for corresponding accelerations a_1 and a_2:

$$\frac{a_1}{a_2} = \frac{p_1}{p_2} = \frac{p_1 \div d}{p_1 \div d} = \frac{\sin A_1}{\sin A_2}$$

The expression on the right is not as Galileo wrote the ratio. Like Stevinus, Galileo used only the language of

* See *Astronomer Priest and Ancient Mariner*, p. 71.

Euclid's geometry. If we write g (as nowadays) for a_2 when $A_2 = 90°$, so that $\sin A_2 = 1$,

$$\frac{a_1}{g} = \sin A_1 \ \ and \ \ a_1 = g \sin A_1$$

It thus turns out that g, which is acceleration for a vertical fall, does not depend on d. At one and the same place it is a constant, being at sea level a velocity increase of approximately 32 feet per second in every second or, as one now writes it, 32 ft. sec^2.

To see what this means, consider two experiments in which the angles of inclination of the planes are respectively $A_1 = 30°$ and $A_2 = 45°$. Since $\sin 30° = 0.5$ and $\sin 45° = 0.707$, the corresponding accelerations will be approximately

$$a_1 = 0.5 \times 32 = 16 \text{ ft sec}^2 \text{ and } a_2 = 0.707 \times 32 = 22.6 \text{ ft sec}^2$$

At this stage of his work, Galileo had provided the materials for a precise definition of force which figures so prominently in the building Newton erected on the foundations he had laid. The statical mechanics of Galileo's predecessors, in particular Archimedes and Stevinus, had measured force in terms of weight without clearly distinguishing between: (a) *mass* which one measures on a balance when two objects, hanging at equal distances from the centre of a lever, are in equilibrium; (b) *force*, exerted by unequal masses in equilibrium when suspended at different distances from the centre of a lever. The statical law of the inclined plane tells us what is the ratio of two balanced unequal masses at rest in the same situation while the dynamical law tells us the ratio of their accelerations if we permit them to move by cutting the connecting cord. We may combine both laws (see p. 76) as follows:

$$\frac{m}{M} = \sin A = \frac{a}{g} \text{ so that } mg = Ma$$

This is a short way of saying: two forces are equal if the product of the mass of one and its acceleration if free to move is equal to the product of the mass of the other and its acceleration if also free to move. This gives us a way of measuring the force, i.e. weight, exerted by a mass both at rest and in motion. It also makes quite explicit the situations in which equal masses and equal weights are not equivalent.

Having determined acceleration under gravity, Galileo next turned his attention to a problem which his fellow countryman Tartaglia had tried, but failed, to solve. At one time a professor of geometry at Brescia, Tartaglia is renowned as the first to solve a cubic equation and to put the imaginary square root of -1 to good use. In 1537 he published a treatise on the theory and practice of gunnery (Fig. 60). He had found empirically that the elevation of a cannon for its greatest range is 45°. Still hidebound by Aristotle's teaching about how bodies fall, he was unable to justify this conclusion theoretically.

60. *Figure from Tartaglia's treatise on artillery mathematics.*

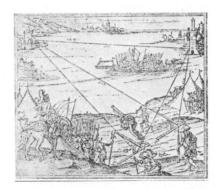

61. *Figure from Zubler's work (1607) on geometric instruments illustrating their use for sighting the target of the cannon ball.*

The foregoing definition of force is one of Newton's three so-called laws of motion. To map the path of the cannon ball, Galileo invoked and transmitted a notion which is another of the same three. This is the principle of *inertia*. One may state it in two ways. One is to define force in a qualitative, as opposed to a quantitative, way as that which changes the speed or direction of motion of a body. Alternatively, one may say that a body remains at rest or continues to move at uniform speed in a straight line in the absence of an applied force, e.g. gravitation or the frictional resistance of the air. It then becomes necessary to distinguish between *crude speed*, i.e. the ratio of distance traversed to time irrespective of the path followed, and *velocity*, i.e. the same ratio if the path does not change its direction in a straight line.

Compounding two motions was not a new intellectual exercise in Galileo's time. It is as old as the observatory temple where the sun's apparent daily course and its annual retreat through the zodiacal constellations were first recognised as concomitant phenomena; but the astronomers of antiquity had learned only to combine two motions (three, if we include *Precession of the Equinoxes*), observed separately one as a daily cycle, the other annual (a third, from Hipparchus onwards of approximately 26,000 years to complete). Galileo compounded two motions which we could see only if one of them could continue without interference from the other. This had no parallel in human experience till man put himself into outer space some four hundred years later.

In making a composite picture (Figs. 62–64) of the track of the cannon ball, Galileo's procedure thus involved a bold innovation. From the principle of inertia, he conceived one component as its initial muzzle velocity in the same straight line as the bore of the cannon at an angle to

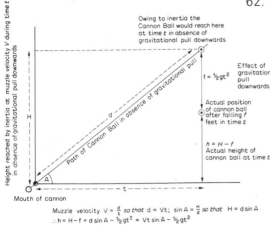

62. *Calculating the Path of the Cannon Ball.*

Owing to inertia the Cannon Ball would reach here at time t in absence of gravitational pull downwards

Height reached by inertia at muzzle velocity V during time t in absence of gravitational pull downwards

Path of Cannon Ball in absence of gravitational pull

$f = \frac{1}{2}gt^2$ Effect of gravitational pull downwards

Actual position of cannon ball after falling f feet in time t

$h = H - f$ Actual height of cannon ball at time t

Mouth of cannon

Muzzle velocity $V = \frac{d}{t}$ so that $d = Vt$; $\sin A = \frac{H}{d}$ so that $H = d \sin A$

$\therefore h = H - f = d \sin A - \frac{1}{2}gt^2 = Vt \sin A - \frac{1}{2}gt^2$

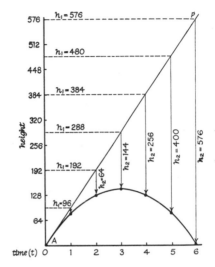

63. *Galileo's interpretation of the parabolic path of the cannon ball.*

$h_1 = 576$

$h_1 = 480$

$h_1 = 384$

$h_1 = 288$

$h_1 = 192$

$h_1 = 96$

height

time (t)

$h_2 = 64$ $h_2 = 144$ $h_2 = 256$ $h_2 = 400$ $h_2 = 576$

plot of $y = x - 8x^2$ (in miles)

max. height 55 yds

range 220 yds

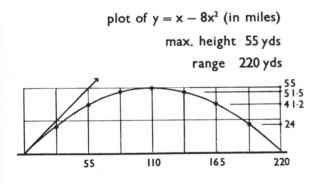

64. *Range and maximum height of Cannon Ball's track.*

the ground determined by its elevation. The other component is its drive vertically downward with constant acceleration by gravitation. As when dealing with the inclined plane, Galileo relied on Euclid's geometry to track the course of the projectile. The reader who is familiar with very elementary graphs will find their use leads less laboriously to the same result—i.e. that the path is the curve called a *parabola*.

From Fig. 62 we see that the connexion between its height (h) at time t with muzzle velocity V from a cannon whose bore makes an angle A with the ground is:

$$h = V. \sin A. t - \tfrac{1}{2}gt^2$$

If $A = 30°$ so that $\sin A = 0.5$, since $g = 32$ ft sec², we get for h in feet

$$h = 0.5 \, V.t - 16 \, t^2$$

This is an equation which describes the curve called a parabola on a graph whose horizontal and vertical axes are respectively t and h. It has two solutions when $h = 0$, i.e. the time at the instant of firing, and the time when it strikes the ground. To get the range R we use the latter value. By definition:

$$\frac{R}{d} = \cos A \quad so \ that \quad R = d \cos A$$

Here $d = Vt$, and if as above $A = 30°$, $\cos A = \tfrac{1}{2}\sqrt{3}$ and $R = \tfrac{1}{2}\sqrt{3} \, Vt$. The only unknown is now V, the muzzle velocity which is measurable from a single determination of R at one fixed angle of elevation. This completes the solution of the problem Tartaglia failed to solve.

The provision of a recipe for finding the range of a cannon given its elevation (A above) and its muzzle velocity was an immense step forward from the standpoint of the military commander in a century when warfare was endemic both in Europe and in the New World. It also set a new problem to the mathematician. To determine the maximum height the cannon ball reaches, and at what distance from its source, was then a matter of moment to the aggressor of a walled city. This problem is one of a larger class which gave impetus to the new (co-ordinate) geometry of Descartes and to the birth of the differential calculus. We may date the latter from Fermat's successful approach to the location of points where a curve reaches its maximum. These two invaluable tools for the study of motion—the one suggested by the track of a ship in latitude and longitude—the other by the highest point in the path of a projectile, had already taken shape during Galileo's old age.

Hitherto, we have been speaking of how bodies fall in air. That the rate at which they fall (or rise) in water depends on their mass was a commonplace of hydrostatics in Galileo's time. If we combine the Archimedean principle of buoyancy with the discovery by Stevinus that the pressure of a liquid at one and the same level is equal in every direction including vertically upwards, we can explain away one difficulty Galileo's critics could advance on the assumption—denied by them—that air has weight. As we shall see in our next chapter, before he was able to prove that air has weight, Galileo had to meet the objection that exceptionally light bodies fall more slowly in air than do comparatively heavy ones.

In his experiments on the inclined plane, a minor source of inaccuracy arose from the frictional resistance between the surfaces of the plane and the balls. It was not necessarily the same if the materials the balls were made of were different. This may have led him to experiment with the pendular swing of different substances. Years before, during a religious service, he had timed against his own pulse-rate the swing of a lamp suspended from the roof of the cathedral in Pisa, and had found that the interval (*period*) of a complete oscillation is constant. Experiment showed that a bob of lead and a cork one of the same size suspended by cords of equal length oscillate through relatively small angles—i.e. not greater than 10° —with equal periods.

Such experiments led Galileo to give instructions to his pupils with a view to constructing a clock with a pendulum regulator (Fig. 65). This invention was a major advance in the technology of time-keeping. Other experiments showed that only two variables determine the time of swing through small angles. The acceleration (g) due to gravity and the length (L) of the cord or rod suspension. If T stands for the time of a complete swing:

$$T = 2\pi\sqrt{\frac{L}{g}}$$

This formula is deducible by considering the tangent at any point on the arc through which the bob swings as an inclined plane.* At one and the same latitude and height above sea level, the value of g is constant. Accordingly, the period then depends only on L. By suspending a button by a long thin piece of cotton of measured length and counting the swings with a watch, the reader can get a good value for g by recourse to the formula above.

Living as we now do in the age of space travel, it may seem difficult to reconcile Galileo's proof that the path of the cannon ball is a parabola with the fact that the path of an artificial satellite is an ellipse. In his proof Galileo assumes, as here, that gravity acts throughout the range of the cannon ball at right angles to the horizon plane. Actually it acts towards the centre of the earth, to which our imaginary horizon plane is tangent. Throughout the relatively short range of the path of the cannon ball in Galileo's time, the assumption he made involves no sensible error. For modern artillery with a vastly greater range, it does. As we increase the height to which a projectile can rise and the distance which it can reach,

* See pp. 286–7 Hogben: *Science for the Citizen* (Third Edition).

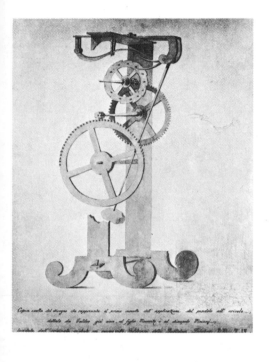

65. *Early model of Pendulum Clock.*

the parabola becomes more and more like an ellipse. As the path bends more and more after reaching its highest point, it eventually passes the point where it can strike the ground. It is then in orbit.

Galileo did not live to see an event which gave the deathblow to what might have seemed to be an immensely important practical consequence of the invention of the pendulum clock and, ironically, a triumphant vindication of his confidence in the Copernican world view. A few years after Galileo died, Picard, a French scientist, made careful observations at Paris to determine the length of a pendulum with a swing of one second. In 1672 another scientist made a similar determination at Cayenne in a French colony on the north coast of South America. On returning to France, he found that his Cayenne pendulum was too short for Paris by about one-tenth of an inch.

To appreciate the explanation of this we must first recall that about 44 degrees separate the latitude of Paris from that of Cayenne. If indeed the earth rotates on its axis, there is therefore a considerable difference between the radius of the circle in which an object at Paris revolves and that of the circle in which an object at Cayenne does so. We may therefore regard the two as placed at the rim of two turntables of different diameters revolving at the same angular speed, i.e. with the same axle. That their diameters are different is important because the force required to prevent a body from flying off the edge of a circular plate revolving at a fixed speed is directly proportional to its diameter. The wider it is, the greater the force.

We next recall that the period (T), i.e. time interval of the complete swing of a pendulum, depends on two variable quantities: its length (L) and the acceleration (g) with which a body falls under the influence of gravity. If the length is greater and g does not change, the period is greater, i.e. the swing is slower. Contrariwise, if the quantity g, already known to decrease with altitude, is greater, the period is shorter and the swing is faster. For a fixed mass, g is our measure of the effective force of gravity pulling bodies towards the earth's centre.

Let us now imagine that we can suspend gravity. If the earth is at rest on its axis, objects at rest on its surface would remain where they are; but if the earth is rotating they would fly off at a tangent unless exactly at the poles, where so-called *centrifugal force* is negligible. Elsewhere, the force required to keep them from doing so depends on the diameter of the circle in which they are moving, i.e. their latitude. It will increase as we approach the equator, being therefore greater at Cayenne (Lat. 5°N) than at Paris (48° 51′N). This must weaken the force pulling towards the earth's centre objects equidistant from it. The effective force of gravity measured by the rate (g) at which falling bodies gain speed must therefore be somewhat less at Cayenne than at Paris.

This signifies that the period of a pendulum of the same length must be longer in Cayenne than in Paris, and shorter in Paris than in Cayenne. If we wish a pendulum with a 1 sec swing in Cayenne to behave in the same way in Paris, we must therefore lengthen it somewhat. A French expedition of 1672 showed that this was so. Huyghens, who gave the earliest satisfactory mathematical treatment of centrifugal force, later showed that gravitational pull varies with latitude in such a way that we can exactly calculate how much effect on the swing of the pendulum a difference of L degrees will make: and observation tallies with the result of the calculation. Thus the hope that the pendulum regulator would be the means of making a "seaworthy" clock proved to be illusory. At the time, this must have seemed to be disappointing from a practical point of view. From a theoretical one, it was not. It had a decisive effect on any lingering scepticism towards the Copernican doctrine that the earth rotates on its own axis.

Though the pendulum thus could not solve the problem of time keeping on sea voyages in different latitudes, it did have one very practical consequence. It placed in the hands of the scientific worker a tool for measuring shorter intervals of time than it had hitherto been possible to do. The second as a time unit ceased to be an abstraction, a circumstance which recalls a discovery dependent on gunnery but not mentioned so far.

During Galileo's lifetime, two Frenchmen, first Gassendi, later Mersenne, made determinations of the speed of sound in air at roughly sea level. Their method was to time the interval between the flash of a cannon and the sound of its explosion at a site of measured distance from it. The implicit assumption of the method is that light traverses space instantaneously. This is not true, but the speed of light is vastly greater than that of sound in any medium. So the error due to the assumption is trivial.

7 **The Third State of Matter**

We have seen how Galileo's treatment of the path of the cannon ball laid the theoretical foundation-stone for the possibility of putting a rocket into orbit. Before he could complete his life work, he had to—and did—dispose of an obstacle which some of Aristotle's predecessors, long since forgotten, had removed. Among the early Greeks, some men of science, in particular Empedocles and Democritus,[1] had held that air has weight; and they did so on the basis of sound reasoning from ingenious observations. Democritus himself had accounted for its compressibility by conceiving that all matter consists of minute particles or, as we now say, molecules, in empty space. Against this, Aristotle claimed that matter exists in only two states: solid and liquid. Air, breath, smoke and vapours, i.e. all that we now speak of as the *gaseous state*, belonged to the weightless domain of *spirits*. To the mediaeval chemist, this term included the human soul. According to the Aristotelian teaching, matter in its two states of solid and liquid had *gravity*, which makes it fall to earth where it belongs. Spirits had *levity* which makes them ascend heavenward.

In Galileo's time, it was already commonplace that whether objects rise or fall in liquids depends solely on relative density. It thus seemed plausible that smoke rises only because it is less dense than air, but such an explanation, which implies that air and smoke have weight, was contrary to Aristotle's doctrine. Against the fact that a cannon ball and a wooden croquet ball, or that balls of either sort if three or four times as large, fall vertically through the same distance in the same time, Galileo's view of gravitation had to find an answer to the question: why does a bladder of the same size and shape as either a

[1] *Astronomer Priest and Ancient Mariner*, pp. 70–71.

cannon ball or a croquet ball when inflated, fall very much more slowly?

If air has weight, this is what we should expect because the density of the inflated bladder must be vastly less than that of any compact solid body of the same size and shape. Moreover air would also offer greater frictional resistance to a falling feather than to a solid body of the same mass on account of its relatively enormous surface. How Galileo set about answering such objections to his own interpretation of how bodies fall we shall here learn in his own words as translated into English from his *Dialogues concerning Two New Sciences*[1] published in 1638 more than forty years after the bulk of the work recorded therein was complete.

There he tells us:

I took a pretty big Glass Bottle, with a narrow Neck, and tied very close to its narrow Neck a Leathern Cover; to this Cover, and within Side, I put a Valve; thr' this with a Syringe I forced a great Quantity of Air, of which, because it admits of great Condensation, twice or thrice as much may be forced in as the Bottle naturally holds: Then I very carefully weigh'd in a most exact Ballance the Bottle with the compressed Air within it, adjusting their Weight by a very fine Sand; then opening the Valve, I let out the Air which was violently contained in the Vessel: I put the Bottle again into the Scales, and finding it much lighter than before, I took out of the other Scales so much Sand (keeping it by itself) until the Sand and the Bottle were *in Equilibrio*: Now there can be no Room to doubt but that the Weight of the Sand taken out is equal to the Weight of the Air which was violently forced into the Bottle, and which afterwards was let out.

But this Experiment assured me of no more than this, *viz.* that the Weight of the Air violently compressed in the Bottle, is equal to the Weight of that reserved Sand: But I have not yet determin'd how much the Air absolutely weighs in respect of Water, or any other heavy Matter; nor can I know this, unless I measure the

[2] trans. by T. Weston, pub. 1730.

Quantity of the compressed Air which may be done by either of
the two ways following.

The former is this: Take such another Bottle, with a Neck
exactly of the same Size with that of the former, round which Neck
tie very fast another Leather, the other End of which tie also
closely over the former Bottle's Neck. Now the Bottom of this
Second Bottle must be drill'd or bor'd thro', so that thro' the Hole
a Wire may be put, wherewith at Pleasure the Valve of the former
Bottle may be open'd to let out the superfluous Air after it hath
been weigh'd. But now this second Bottle must be fill'd with
Water. All things thus prepar'd, and the Valve open'd by Help
of the Wire, the Air issuing out with Impetuosity, and entering the
Bottle of Water, shall drive the Water out by the Hole at the
Bottom. Now 'tis manifest that the Quantity of Water forc'd out
in this manner, is = the Bulk and Quantity of Air that issued out
of the other Bottle; Wherefore keeping that Water let the Bottle,
now lighten'd of the compressed Air be again weigh'd, (for I
suppose it to have been weigh'd before, together with the compressed Air) and then 'tis manifest that the superfluous Sand,
reserv'd as before order'd, is exactly equal to the Weight of such a
Mass of Air, as is the Mass of Water forc'd out and preserv'd,
which, if weigh'd, we shall see how many times its Weight shall
contain the Weight of the reserv'd Sand; and we may safely
affirm, that the Water is so much heavier than the Air, which will
not be only ten times, as seems to be *Aristotle's* Opinion, but
nearly 400 times, as this Experiment shows us.

The other Method is more expeditious, and by making use of
one Vessel only; and that is the former fitted as before directed,
excepting that I would have no more Air in it than what is naturally
in it; but I would have Water injected without letting out the
least Air, which being forced to give way to the supervenient
Water, must of Necessity be compress'd: Having gotten in as much
Water as possible, (which without much Force may be about three
Fourths of what the Bottle will hold) put it into the Scales, and
weigh it very exactly; which done, holding the Vessel with the
Neck upwards, and opening the Valve, let the Air out, of which
there will issue such a Quantity as there is Water in the Bottle.
The Air being gone out, put the Vessel again into the Scales, which,
because of the Air let out, will be found lighter; and taking out of
the other Scale the Over-weight, it will give us the Weight of such
a Mass of Air as is that of the Water in the Bottle.

In the light of the work of Archimedes on buoyancy, Galileo then proceeds to deal with whether the air itself gravitates. To show that it does so:

We must chuse a Place and *Medium* where the Air, as well as the Sand, may do so; because, as has been often said, the *Medium* takes off from the Weight of every Matter immers'd therein, so much as in the Weight of a Mass of the same *Medium*, which is = the immersed Mass; so that I can't deny but that the Air depriveth the Air of all its Gravity. The Experiment therefore ought to be tried in a *Vacuum*, where all Bodies would exercise their Faculties without any Diminution: Wherefore, if we weigh any Portion of Air in a Vacuum, would you then be convinc'd in this Matter?

We may better appreciate this argument, if we re-interpret Archimedes' principle in terms of the new measure of *Force* which emerges from Galileo's own experiments on motion down an inclined surface (p. 83). If we use Galileo's measure of weight as the product of mass and acceleration if free to fall, we can infer the principle of buoyancy from the observed fact (p. 79) that fluid pressure is the same if communicated both up-wards and downwards. If M is the mass of a cylinder (Fig. 66) of density D in air, it would weigh in water (density d)

$$m = M\left(1 - \frac{d}{D}\right) \ and \ \frac{m}{M} = 1 - \frac{d}{D}$$

If fully immersed, when its descent is balanced by the upward thrust of the water, we have two forces in equilib-rium, a being its acceleration if free to fall vertically in the water:

$$mg = M.a \ so \ that \ \frac{a}{g} = \frac{m}{M}$$

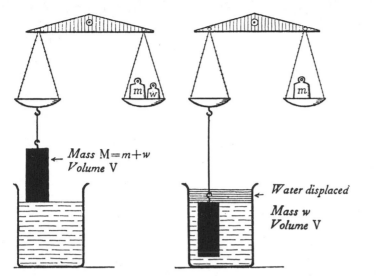

Mass M=m+w
Volume V

Water displaced
Mass w
Volume V

66. *Experimental proof of formula connecting the acceleration of a submerged body with its density and that of the liquid.*

The Archimedean principle states that a body of mass M, density D and volume V immersed in a liquid of density d if suspended from one arm of a balance is in equilibrium with another suspended from the other arm in air if its mass is less than M by the mass m of an equivalent volume of liquid. By definition,

$$D = \frac{M}{V} \text{ and } d = \frac{m}{V}$$

so that $M = VD$ and $m = Vd$.

If the mass M when free to fall in the liquid had an acceleration a in the liquid and the masses M and m when free to fall in air have an acceleration g, they will balance when

$$Ma = Mg - mg$$

so that $Vda = (VD - Vd) g$

$$\therefore a = \left(1 - \frac{d}{D}\right) g.$$

For example, if we take the density of iron as approximately 8 times that of water:

$$\frac{a}{g} = 1 - \frac{1}{8} = 0.875$$

Thus an iron body will fall in water with an acceleration approximately 0.875 g and, if we take $g = 32$ ft per sec^2, at approximately 29 ft per sec^2. If we take for illustrative purposes, Galileo's own estimate that water is 400 times as dense as air:

$$\frac{a}{g} = 1 - \frac{1}{8 \times 400} = 0.9996 \text{ and } a = 0.9996 \, g$$

Thus the iron will fall in air with an acceleration almost exactly the same as in a vacuum. Now suppose we replace the cylinder by an inflated bladder of density less than one two-hundredth of the density of water, i.e. on Galileo's estimate a density twice that of air, we obtain

$$\frac{a}{g} = 1 - \frac{1}{2} \text{ so that } a = 0.5 \, g$$

So our inflated bladder will fall with an acceleration in air only half as great as *in vacuo* and about half that of an iron body of the same shape and size in air.

Till Galileo's time, his predecessors had explained

suction phenomena, such as the rise of water in the shaft of a pump, by saying that *nature abhors a vacuum*. He himself was seemingly familiar with Agricola's relays of pumps (Fig. 67), since he drew attention to the fact that the weight of the air could not lift a column of water more than about 32 feet above its external level. In other

67. *A woodcut from Agricola's treatise on mining technology showing relays of pumps necessary because the weight of the air can raise water only about 30 ft.*

words, as Pledge puts it, "nature abhors a vacuum only up to a certain point". This consideration led Galileo's pupil Torricelli to test to what height the alleged abhorrence of a vacuum would raise a column of mercury. Mercury is about 14 times as dense as water. Therefore he expected that the length of a column of mercury which would balance the weight of the air would be about one fourteenth of the length of a column of water able to do the same. His colleague Viviani confirmed the surmise. In the year of Galileo's death, Torricelli and

Viviani reported joint experiments (Fig. 68) of which the
outcome was the type of simple barometer made by filling
a tube with mercury, closing the aperture with a finger
tip and inverting it vertically in a bowl of mercury. If
the tube is sufficiently long, the mercury in it falls till
the height of the column above the level of mercury in the
bowl is about 31 inches, how nearly depending on the
atmospheric pressure at the time and place. Since no air
had access to the empty space above the column, here at
last was a true vacuum.

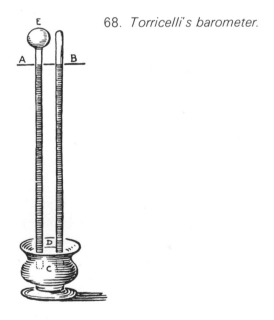

68. *Torricelli's barometer.*

To produce a vacuum by suction set the contemporaries
of Torricelli and Viviani a new technological problem. To
be effective it called for a more reliable valve than any
pump then in use. The exact date at which it was possible
to produce one with a pump is uncertain because its
inventor, a German named von Guericke, did not publish
the results of extensive experiments till much later (Fig.
69). It is probable, however, that he had completed most
of them by the year (1642) in which Galileo died. Among

them was one for which he designed two hollow bronze hemispheres whose flattened edges fitted securely when he evacuated the composite vessel provided with a stop-cock. So long as the stopcock remained closed, the pressure of the air on the outside defied any attempt to separate the hemispherical halves even when two teams of eight horses harnessed to opposite halves pulled their hardest in opposite directions (Fig. 70). Public demonstration of his experiments did not occur till 1654, twelve years after the death of Galileo; but vindication of the usefulness of the invention of an air pump as a passport to discovery probably happened in Galileo's lifetime.

One result was to give the study of sound a new foothold. It had been known from time immemorial that sound is produced by vibrations of stretched strings, as of a harp and, after the Christian church had nursed into being the monastery organ, that it is also due to pulsating columns of air. Galileo himself had made experiments on producing different musical notes by scratching a metal bar at regular intervals of different length. That air is the medium through which our ears receive sounds was not alien to mediaeval thinking, but there was no proof of it. The road was now clear to an understanding of how the medium transmits the impact of the initial vibration of string, bell, tuning fork or pipe, etc.

Guericke gave us the tool to finish the job. By enclosing a bell with a clockwork mechanism to keep it ringing in a glass vessel having a stopcock, one can show that the sound becomes less audible, and eventually silent, as one proceeds to evacuate the container. On readmission of air it becomes audible once more. This demonstration led to the wave theory of sound propagation. Because the bell remains visible throughout, we also learn that light, unlike sound, does not need air—or other transparent

69. *Guericke's second air pump.*

material—for its transmission.

Though other inventions of the sixteenth and early seventeenth centuries have exerted greater influence in the long run, it is scarcely too much to say that none had a greater impact on human curiosity than had the air pump in the twenty years following the death of Galileo and the birth of Newton. It added final confirmation of Galileo's doctrine of terrestrial gravitation when it was possible for Newton to demonstrate that a gold coin and a feather descend at the same rate in a long transparent tube evacuated of all air, and it confirmed in a new way that air has weight when Boyle set up a barometer in a vessel connected to an air pump so that the mercury column fell as the air pressure also fell.

During the lifetime of Galileo, a Flemish physician, van Helmont, seems to have been the only person who had any clear notion of what the recognition of the third state of matter could mean to the as yet unborn sciences of chemistry and physiology. To him we owe the substitution of the neutral word *gas* for spirits and for all the mystical associations which clung to the latter. Van Helmont

70. *Guericke's experiment with the 'Magdeburg Hemispheres'.*

recognised that there are many different sorts of air, as so-called for several generations later, i.e. as we now say, there are many different substances which exist in the gaseous state. He demonstrated by experiment that growing plants draw from the air around them a weighable material. We now call it carbon dioxide. He called it *gas sylvestre*.

Van Helmont's work did not become available to his countrymen till four years after he died, and first became available by translations abroad during the sixties and early seventies of the same century. In these decades Boyle, Hooke and Mayow in England gave the study of combustion, of respiration and of the extraction of metals from their ores a promising but abortive new impetus. To Boyle's *Sceptical Chemist* (1661), and to his German teacher Jung who advanced similar views in 1634, we owe the first hint of a modern definition of an element replacing the sacred four (earth, air, fire, water) of Aristotle. Boyle and Hooke, more than any of their contemporaries, were responsible for introducing scientific investigators to the atomic speculations of the early Greek materialists.

In England, Boyle and Hooke used and greatly improved

the vacuum pump within a generation after the death of Galileo. They recorded that small animals suffocated in the partial vacuum of a vessel attached to it, that a candle flame went blue and soon went out, and that glowing coal lost its redness, though a pistol primed with gunpowder could still discharge in a vacuum. Such enquiries might have immediately revolutionised chemistry had there not been a revival of Aristotle's teaching in Germany where the elemental fire of the ancients came to life again, and now endowed with levity, as *phlogiston*.

Otherwise, the way was clear for getting answers to two questions raised by Agricola's volume on the health hazards of miners: why is some "air" inflammable and why does not some "air" sustain respiration? An answer to the first of these two questions was not available till nearly three centuries after the *De Re Metallica* appeared in print; but Hooke indeed did show that air enclosed in a glass vessel inverted over water, if rendered unfit for combustion or respiration by burning a candle in it, can be rendered fit for burning or breathing by heating *nitre* (potassium nitrate) therein. Nitre, as we now know, liberated oxygen in place of what has been converted into carbon dioxide. Applying the teachings of Democritus, lately disseminated by Gassendi's translations of Epicurus, Hooke rightly drew the conclusion that air consists of two sorts of particles, i.e. one sort necessary to maintain combustion and respiration (i.e. oxygen), the other inert (what we now call nitrogen). Contemporary chemists, steeped in Aristotle's mystique, failed to recognise the significance of this discovery. Until Lavoisier dealt the death-blow to phlogiston a century later, they were not ready to respond as they did when Dalton subsequently revived the doctrine of Democritus, i.e. that all matter consists of minute particles.

Though chemists in Hooke's time continued to oppose such a view, it found a hearing among those who realised more fully the implications of the fact that air has weight. If so, its density and compressibility are inexorably connected; and the possibility that it consists of invisible particles widely apart in empty space offers an intelligible explanation of its compressibility. It was for Hooke and Boyle to formulate what has proved to be the keystone of modern physical chemistry. This is the law that the volume of a gas at constant temperature is inversely proportional to the pressure applied.

If chemists were slow to respond to the theoretical possibilities of the discovery that air is a third state of matter, it opened up a vast horizon of discovery in readiness for the recognition of atoms and molecules at a much later date, and, in the meantime, a new understanding of how to make compounds. So much is clear, if we recall the composition of the main ingredients of manufacturing processes other than metallurgical before chemical industries began in the period 1750–1800. Chalk and potash are each a compound of a gas and two solid elements, saltpetre and slaked lime each of a metal and two gaseous elements.

One might continue in this vein. It suffices to say that the apothecary, who was the purveyor of pure substances other than gold, silver and diamonds, could have no intelligible guidance to mixing in their right proportions the right ingredients of any manufactured substitute for a crude raw material before he recognised that air has weight, that it is a mixture (mainly) of two of a vast number of other substances which exist at ordinary temperatures in the gaseous state and that each such gas at a fixed pressure and temperature has its own characteristic density. At a time when the study of combustion and respiration were closely knit, physiology set itself a new goal and some medical men, less hide-bound than apothecaries, played an important role in the exploration of the gaseous state.

The role of the air pump in the study of sound, as mentioned above, recalls discoveries made in the context of newly invented musical instruments (p. 26). Galileo himself established the numerical relation between frequency of vibration of a stretched cord and the pitch of the note emitted by it. Stimulated by Galileo's work, Mersenne (p. 91) discovered that a vibrating string produces overtones in addition to the fundamental note. He also explored the relation between the frequency of vibration and the length, diameter and density of a string stretched by different weights, also the effect of such differences.

As we conclude the story of how science began, it is fitting to contrast the accumulation of scientific knowledge before and during the life-span (1564–1642) of Galileo. Before his birth, its major achievements were based on observation alone, including especially descriptive astronomy and scientific geography. Generalisations based on experiment were few: the relation of the length of the same cord stretched by equal weights to the note it emits, the construction of images by reflection of light, the law of the lever and of buoyancy in liquids. To be just to antiquity, one should also recall that Ptolemy (p. 73) and his contemporaries performed experiments on refraction of light from air to water. However, they discovered no general rule.

If we date the beginning of natural science as from the start of the Egyptian calendar based on a *sidereal* (Sirius) year, the foregoing list embraces the total output of experimental, as opposed to observational, science during some five thousand years before the birth of Galileo. When he died, the principles of hydrostatics, the law of refraction and the recipe for image formation by lenses, the fundamental laws of acoustics and the law of terrestrial gravitation had been established. The tool-kit of the scientific worker now included the microscope, the telescope, the barometer and the air pump. Galileo himself had set the stage for the study of heat by devising a simple thermometer. Meanwhile, the proof that air has weight had disclosed a vast vista for future experimental study of chemical combination in general and respiration in particular.